The Cotswolds

Kirsty Holmes

Credits

Footprint credits
Editor: Sophie Jones
Production and layout: Emma Bryers
Maps: Kevin Feeney
Cover: Pepi Bluck

Publisher: Patrick Dawson
Managing Editor: Felicity Laughton
Advertising: Elizabeth Taylor
Sales and marketing: Kirsty Holmes

Photography credits
Front cover: stocker1970/Shutterstock.com
Back cover: Antb/Shutterstock.com

Printed in Great Britain by CPI Antony Rowe, Chippenham, Wiltshire

MIX
Paper from
responsible sources
FSC
www.fsc.org
FSC® C013604

Every effort has been made to ensure that the facts in this guidebook are accurate. However, travellers should still obtain advice from consulates, airlines, etc, about travel and visa requirements before travelling. The authors and publishers cannot accept responsibility for any loss, injury or inconvenience however caused.

Contains Ordnance Survey data © Crown copyright and database right 2013

Publishing information
Footprint *Focus The Cotswolds*
1st edition
© Footprint Handbooks Ltd
April 2013

ISBN: 978 1 908206 99 2
CIP DATA: A catalogue record for this book is available from the British Library

® Footprint Handbooks and the Footprint mark are a registered trademark of Footprint Handbooks Ltd

Published by Footprint
6 Riverside Court
Lower Bristol Road
Bath BA2 3DZ, UK
T +44 (0)1225 469141
F +44 (0)1225 469461
footprinttravelguides.com

Distributed in the USA by Globe Pequot Press, Guilford, Connecticut

The content of Footprint *Focus The Cotswolds* has been updated from Footprint's *England Handbook*, which was researched and written by Charlie Godfrey Fausset.

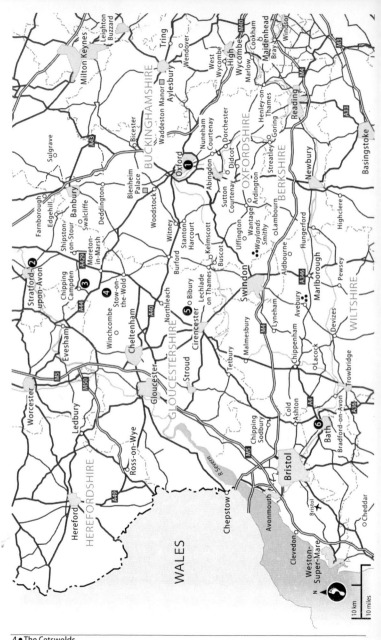

The gentle limestone hills and valleys of the Cotswolds spread across a swathe of Gloucestershire and into surrounding counties. Designated an Area of Outstanding Natural Beauty, the Cotswolds conjure up images of quintessential England: rolling hills, honey-coloured stone cottages and sleepy villages. The region is overwhelmed with admirers every summer and many of its genteel villages pander to a nostalgic vision of England past. That said, their immaculate state of preservation and the apparently organic way they seem to have grown up from the soil makes them truly irresistible. Small boutique hotels and gastropubs cater for the area's well-heeled visitors, providing havens of luxury and the chance to sample the high-quality local produce. This is also superb walking country, and the tourist hordes can easily be escaped on foot or bike along quiet river valleys.

Around the edges of the Cotswolds are some of Britain's most famous and most stunning cities: Oxford, to the east, is one of the most celebrated academic hubs in the world, and it's easy to see why it continues to charm people from around the globe. To the north is Stratford-upon-Avon, a mecca for history and theatre buffs, while to the south is Bath, a glorious spa town that has enamoured visitors for centuries. On the western edge of the Cotswolds, Cheltenham and Gloucester are two cities with very different personalities that provide a refreshing urban balance to the countryside.

Planning your trip

Best time to visit England

The weather in England is generally better between May and September, although it can be gloriously hot in April and cold and damp in August. The west of the country is milder and wetter than the east, whilst northern regions and mountainous areas such as the Peninnes are usually the coldest areas.

Transport in England

Compared to the rest of Western Europe, public transport in England is not always reliable and can be expensive. Rail travel, in particular can be very pricey unless booked well in advance. Coach travel is cheaper but much slower, and is further hampered by serious traffic problems around London, Manchester and Birmingham. Some areas, such as the Cotswolds, Peak or Lake District, are poorly served by public transport of any kind, and if you plan to spend much time in rural areas, it may be worth hiring a car, especially if you are travelling as a couple or group. A useful website for all national public transport information is **Traveline** ① *T0871-200 2233, www.traveline.info*.

Air
England is a small country, and air travel isn't strictly necessary to get around. However, with traffic a problem around the cities, some of the cheap fares offered by budget airlines may be very attractive. There are good connections between **London** and all the regional airports, although travel from region to region without coming through London is more difficult and expensive. Bear in mind the time and money it will take you to get to the airport (including check in times) when deciding whether flying is really going to be a better deal.

Airport information **National Express** operates a frequent service between London's main airports. **London Heathrow Airport** ① *16 miles west of London between junctions 3 and 4 on the M4, T0844-335 1801, www.heathrowairport.com*, is the world's busiest international airport and it has five terminals, so when leaving London, it's important to check which terminal to go to before setting out for the airport. To get into central London, the cheapest option is the London Underground Piccadilly Line (50 minutes). The fastest option is **Heathrow Express** ① *T0845-600 1515, www.heathrowexpress.com*, taking 15-20 minutes. There is a train service **Heathrow Connect** ① *Heathrow T0845-748 4950, www.heathrow connect.com*, which takes 25 minutes. Coaches to destinations all over the country are run by **National Express** ① *T0871-781 8181, www.nationalexpress. com*. There are also buses to Oxford (www.oxfordbus.co.uk), to Reading for trains to Bristol and southwest England (www.railair.com), to Watford for trains to the north of England (www.greenline.co.uk) and to West London (www.tfl.gov.uk). A taxi to central London takes one hour and costs £45-£70.
    London Gatwick Airport ① *28 miles south of London, off junction 9 on the M23, T0844-892 03222, www.gatwickairport.com*, has two terminals, North and South, with all the usual facilities. To central London, there is the **Gatwick Express** ① *T0845-850 1530, www.*

Don't miss...

1 **Punting along the rivers Cherwell or Isis in Oxford**, page 37.
2 **Seeing the Bard's work brought to life at the Royal Shakespeare Theatre in Stratford**, page 41.
3 **Walking part of the Cotswold Way from Chipping Campden**, page 52.
4 **Visiting the eccentric collections and beautiful gardens at Snowshill Manor**, page 53.
5 **Enjoying the luxury and gastronomy at a Cotswold boutique hotel**, pages 62-65.
6 **Rubbing shoulders with Roman goddesses and restorative minerals at the Roman Baths**, page 73.

Numbers relate to the map on page 4.

---

gatwickexpress.com, from £17.75 single online, which takes 30 minutes. **Thameslink** rail services run from King's Cross, Farringdon, Blackfriars and London Bridge stations. Contact **National Rail Enquiries** ① *T0845-748 4950, www.nationalrail.co.uk*, for further information. **EasyBus** (www.easybus.co.uk) is the cheapest option, with prices at £9.99 single, taking just over an hour. A taxi takes a similar time and costs from around £60.

London City Airport ① *Royal Dock, 6 miles (15 mins' drive) east of the City of London, T020-7646 0000, www.londoncityairport.com*. Take the **Docklands Light Railway** (DLR) to Canning Town (seven minutes) for the **Jubilee line** or a connecting shuttle bus service. A taxi into central London will cost around £35.

London Luton Airport ① *30 miles north of central London, 2 miles off the M1 at junction 10, southeast of Luton, Beds, T01582-405100, www.london-luton.co.uk*. Regular **First Capital Connect** trains run to central London; a free shuttle bus service operates between the airport terminal and the station. **Green Line** ① *www.greenline.co.uk*, coaches run to central London, as does **easyBus** ① *www.easybus.co.uk*. **National Express** ① *www.nationalexpress. com*, operate coaches to many destinations. A taxi takes 50 minutes, costing from £70.

Stansted Airport ① *35 miles northeast of London (near Cambridge) by junction 8 of the M11, T0844-335 1803, www.stanstedairport.com*. **Stansted Express** ① *T0845-600 7245, www.stanstedexpress.com*, runs trains to London's Liverpool Street Station (45 minutes, £22.50 single). **EasyBus** ① *www.easybus.co.uk, from £2*, **Terravision** ① *www.terravision.eu, £9*, and **National Express** ① *www.nationalexpress.com, from £8.50*, run to central London (55 minutes to East London, 1 hour 30 minutes to Victoria). A taxi to central London takes around an hour to 1 hour 30 minutes, depending on traffic, and costs around £99.

Manchester International Airport ① *at junction 5 of the M56, T0871-271 0711, www. manchester airport.co.uk*. The airport is well-served by public transport, with trains to and from Manchester Piccadilly as well as direct and connecting services from all over the north of England. **National Express** ① *www.nationalexpress.com*, runs routes covering the whole of the UK. A taxi into the city centre should cost around £20.

Birmingham International Airport (BHX) ① *8 miles east of the city centre at junction 6 on the M42, T0871-222 0072, www.birminghamairport.co.uk*. A taxi into the centre should cost from £25. Several trains per hour run the free 10-minute Air-Rail Link to Birmingham International Station, and other connections across England and Wales can be made by rail or coach, with **National Express** ① *www.nationalexpress.com*.

Rail

National Rail Enquiries ① *T08457-484950, www.nationalrail.co.uk*, are quick and courteous with information on rail services and fares but not always accurate, so double check. They can't book tickets but will provide you with the relevant telephone number. The website, www.thetrainline.co.uk, also shows prices clearly.

Railcards There are a variety of railcards which give discounts on fares for certain groups. Cards are valid for one year and most are available from main stations. You need two passport photos and proof of age or status. A Young Person's Railcard is for those aged 16-25 or full-time students aged 26+ in the UK. Costs £28 for one year and gives 33% discount on most train tickets and some other services (www.16-25railcard.co.uk). A Senior Citizen's Railcard is for those aged over 60, is the same price and offers the same discounts as a Young Person's Railcard (www.senior-railcard.co.uk). A Disabled Person's Railcard costs £20 and gives 33% discount to a disabled person and one other. Pick up an application form from stations and send it to Disabled Person's Railcard Office, PO Box 11631, Laurencekirk AB30 9AA. It may take up to 10 working days to be delivered, so apply in advance (www.disabledpersons-railcard.co.uk). A Family & Friends Railcard costs £28 and gives 33% discount on most tickets for up to four adults travelling together, and 60% discount for up to four children. It's available to buy online as well as in most stations.

Road

Bus and coach Travelling by bus takes longer than the train but is much cheaper. Road links between cities and major towns in England are excellent, but far less frequent in more remote rural areas, and a number of companies offer express coach services day and night. The main operator is **National Express** ① *T08717-818178, www.national express. com*, which has a nationwide network with over 1000 destinations. Tickets can be bought at bus stations, from a huge number of agents throughout the country or online. Sample return fares if booked in advance: London to Manchester (four hours 35 minutes) £28, London to Cambridge (two hours 30 minutes) £12. **Megabus** ① *T0900-1600 900 (61p a min from BT landlines, calls from other networks may be higher), http://megabus.com*, is a cheaper alternative with a more limited service.

Full-time students, those aged under 25 or over 60 or those registered disabled, can buy a **coach card** for £10 which is valid for one year and gets you a 30% discount on all fares. Children normally travel for half price, but with a Family Card costing £16, two children travel free with two adults. Available to overseas passport holders, the **Brit Xplorer Pass** offers unlimited travel on all National Express buses. Passes cost from £79 for seven days, £139 for 14 days and £219 for its month-long Rolling Stone pass. They can be bought from major airports and bus terminals.

Car Travelling with your own private transport is the ideal way to explore the country, particularly in areas badly served by public transport. This allows you to cover a lot of ground in a short space of time and to reach remote places. The main disadvantages are rising fuel costs, parking and traffic congestion. The latter is particularly heavy on the M25 which encircles London, the M6 around Birmingham and the M62 around Manchester. The M4 and M5 motorways to the West Country can also become choked at weekends and bank holidays and the roads in Cornwall often resemble a glorified car park during the summer.

Motoring organizations can help with route planning, traffic advice, insurance and breakdown cover. The two main ones are: the **Automobile Association (AA)** ① *T0800-085 2721, emergency number T0800-887766, www.theaa.com*, which offers a year's breakdown cover starting at £38, and the **Royal Automobile Club (RAC)** ① *T0844-273 4341, emergency number T08000-828282, www.rac.co.uk*, which has a year's breakdown cover starting at £31.99. Both have cover for emergency assistance. You can still call the emergency numbers if you're not a member, but you'll have to a pay a large fee.

Vehicle hire

Car hire is expensive and the minimum you can expect to pay is around £100 per week for a small car. Always check and compare conditions, such as mileage limitations, excess payable in the case of an accident, etc. Small, local hire companies often offer better deals than the larger multinationals. Most companies prefer payment with a credit card – some insist on it – otherwise you'll have to leave a large deposit (£100 or more). You need to have had a full driver's licence for at least a year and to be aged between 21 (25 for some companies) and 70.

Bicycle

Cycling is a pleasant if slightly hazardous way to see the country. Although conditions for cyclists are improving, with a growing network of cycle lanes in cities, most other roads do not have designated cycle paths, and cyclists are not allowed on motorways. You can load your bike onto trains, though some restrictions apply during rush hour. See www.ctc.org. uk for information on routes, restrictions and facilities.

Where to stay in England

Accommodation can mean anything from being pampered to within an inch of your life in a country house spa hotel to glamping in a yurt. If you have the money, then the sky is very much the limit in terms of sheer splendour and excess. We have listed top class establishments in this book, with a bias towards those that offer that little bit extra in terms of character.

We have tried to give as broad a selection as possible to cater for all tastes and budgets but if you can't find what you're after, or if someone else has beaten you to the draw, then the tourist information centres (TICs) will help find accommodation for you. Some offices charge a small fee (usually £1) for booking a room, while others ask you to pay a deposit of 10% which is deducted from your first night's bill. Details of town and city TICs are given throughout the guide.

Accommodation will be your greatest expense, particularly if you are travelling on your own. Single rooms are in short supply and many places are reluctant to let a double room to one person, even when they're not busy. Single rooms are usually more than the cost per person for a double room and sometimes cost the same as two people sharing a double room.

Hotels, guesthouses and B&Bs

Area tourist boards publish accommodation lists that include campsites, hostels, self-catering accommodation, hotels, guesthouses and bed and breakfasts (B&Bs). Places participating in the VisitEngland system will have a plaque displayed outside which shows their grading, determined by a number of stars ranging from one to five. These reflect the level of facilities, as well as the quality of hospitality and service. However, do not assume that a B&B, guesthouse or hotel is no good because it is not listed by the tourist board. They simply don't want to pay to be included in the system, and some of them may offer better value.

Hotels At the top end of the scale there are some fabulously luxurious hotels, some in beautiful locations. Some are converted mansions or castles, and offer a chance to enjoy a taste of aristocratic grandeur and style. At the lower end of the scale, there is often little to choose between cheaper hotels and guesthouses or B&Bs. The latter often offer higher standards of comfort and a more personal service, but many smaller hotels are really just guesthouses, and are often family run and every bit as friendly. Rooms in most mid-range to expensive hotels almost always have bathrooms en suite. Many upmarket hotels offer excellent room-only deals in the low season. An efficient last-minute hotel booking service is www.laterooms.com, which specializes in weekend breaks. Also note that many hotels offer cheaper rates for online booking through agencies such as www.lastminute.com.

Guesthouses Guesthouses are often large, converted family homes with up to five or six rooms. They tend to be slightly more expensive than B&Bs, charging between £30 and £50 per person per night, and though they are often less personal, usually provide better facilities, such as en suite bathroom, TV in each room, free Wi-Fi and private parking. Many guesthouses offer evening meals, though this may have to be requested in advance.

Bed and breakfasts (B&Bs) B&Bs usually provide the cheapest private accommodation. At the bottom end of the scale you can get a bedroom in a private house, a shared bathroom

Price codes

Where to stay

££££ over £160	£££ £90-160
££ £50-90	£ under £50

Prices include taxes and service charge, but not meals. They are based on one night in a double room in high season.

Restaurants

£££ over £30	££ £15-30	£ under £15

Prices refer to the cost of a two-course meal for one person, without a drink.

and a huge cooked breakfast from around £25 per person per night. Small B&Bs may only have one or two rooms to let, so it's important to book in advance during the summer season. More upmarket B&Bs, some in handsome period houses, have en suite bathrooms, free Wi-Fi and TVs in each room and usually charge from £35 per person per night.

Hostels

For those travelling on a tight budget, there is a network of hostels offering cheap accommodation in major cities, national parks and other areas of beauty, run by the **Youth Hostel Association (YHA)** ① *T01629-592600, or customer services T0800-0191 700*, T+44-1629 592700 from outside the UK, www.yha.org.uk. Membership costs from £14.35 a year and a bed in a dormitory costs from £15 to £25 a night. They offer bunk-bed accommodation in single-sex dormitories or smaller rooms, as well as family rooms, kitchen and laundry facilities. Though some rural hostels are still strict on discipline and impose a 2300 curfew, those in larger towns and cities tend to be more relaxed and doors are closed as late as 0200. Some larger hostels provide breakfasts for around £2.50 and three-course evening meals for £4-5. You should always phone ahead, as many hostels are closed during the day and phone numbers are listed in this guide. Advance booking is recommended at all times, particularly from May to September and on public holidays. Many hostels are closed during the winter. Youth hostel members are entitled to various discounts, including tourist attractions and travel. The YHA also offer budget self-catering bunkhouses with mostly dorm accommodation and some family rooms, which are in more rural locations. Camping barns, camping pods and camping are other options offered by the YHA; see the website for details.

Details of most independent hostels can be found in the *Independent Hostel Guide* (T01629-580427, www.independenthostelguide.co.uk). Independent hostels tend to be more laid-back, with fewer rules and no curfew, and no membership is required. They all have dorms, hot showers and self-catering kitchens, and some have family and double rooms. Some include continental breakfast, or offer cheap breakfasts.

Self-catering accommodation

There are lots of different types of accommodation to choose from, to suit all budgets, ranging from luxury lodges, castles and lighthouses to basic cottages. Expect to pay at least £200-400 per week for a two-bedroom cottage in the winter, rising to £400-1000 in the high season, or more if it's a particularly nice place. A good source of information on self-catering accommodation is the VisitEngland website, www.visitengland.com, and its *VisitEngland Self-catering 2013* guide, which lists many properties and is available to buy from any tourist office and many bookshops, but there are also dozens of excellent websites to browse. Amongst the best websites are: www.cottages4you.co.uk, www.ruralretreats.co.uk and www.ownersdirect.co.uk. If you want to tickle a trout or feed a pet lamb, **Farm Stay UK** ⓘ *www.farmstay.co.uk*, offer over a thousand good value rural places to stay around England, all clearly listed on a clickable map.

More interesting places to stay are offered by the **Landmark Trust** ⓘ *T01628-825925, www.landmarktrust.org.uk*, who rent out renovated historic landmark buildings, from atmospheric castles to cottages, and the **National Trust** ⓘ *T0844-800 2070, www.nationaltrustcottages.co.uk*, who provide a wide variety of different accommodation on their estates. A reputable agent for self-catering cottages is **English Country Cottages** ⓘ *T0845-268 0785, www.english-country-cottages.co.uk*.

Campsites

Campsites vary greatly in quality and level of facilities. Some sites are only open from April to October. See the following sites: www.pitchup.com; www.coolcamping.com, good for finding characterful sites that allow campfires; www.ukcampsite.co.uk, which is the most comprehensive service with thousands of sites, many with pictures and reviews from punters; and www.campingandcaravanningclub.co.uk. The Forestry Commission have campsites on their wooded estates, see www.campingintheforest.com.

Food and drink in England

Food

Only 30 years ago few would have thought to come to England for haute cuisine. Since the 1980s, though, the English have been determinedly shrugging off their reputation for over-boiled cabbage and watery beef. Now cookery shows like Masterchef are the most popular on TV after the soaps, and thanks in part to the wave of celebrity chefs they have created, you can expect a generally high standard of competence in restaurant kitchens. Towns like Ludlow, Padstow and Whitstable have carved reputations for themselves almost solely on the strength of their cuisine.

Pub food has also been transformed in recent years, and now many of them offer ambitious lunchtime and supper menus in so-called gastro pubs. Most parts of the country still boast regional specialities, including succulent Colchester oysters and Cromer crabs. Other specialities are spankingly fresh seafood, especially oysters, winkles, and mussels Norfolk, as well as fish from the sea – often bass, mullet and sole – and from the farm – trout and salmon, mainly.

The biggest problem with eating out is the ludicrously limited serving hours in some pubs and hotels, particularly in remoter locations. These places only serve food during restricted hours, generally about 1200-1430 for lunch and 1830-2130 for supper, seemingly ignorant of the eating habits of foreign visitors, or those who would prefer a bit more flexibility during their holiday. In small places especially, it can be difficult finding food outside these enforced times. Places that serve food all day till 2100 or later are restaurants, fast-food outlets and the many chic bistros and café-bars, which can be found not only in the main cities but increasingly in smaller towns. The latter often offer very good value and above-average quality fare.

Drink

Drinking is a national hobby and sometimes a dangerous one at that. **Real ale** – flat, brown **beer** known as **bitter**, made with hops – is the national drink, but now struggles to maintain its market share in the face of fierce competition from continental lagers and alcopops. Many small independent breweries are still up and running though, as well as microbreweries attached to individual **pubs**, which produce far superior ales. **Cider** (fermented apple juice) is also experiencing a resurgence of interest and is a speciality of Somerset. English **wine** is also proving surprisingly resilient: generally it compares favourably with German varieties and many vineyards now offer continental-style sampling sessions.

In many pubs the basic ales are chilled under gas pressure like lagers, but the best ales, such as those from the independents, are 'real ales', still fermenting in the cask and served cool but not chilled (around 12°C) under natural pressure from a handpump, electric pump or air pressure fount.

The **pub** is still the traditional place to enjoy a drink: the best are usually freehouses (not tied to a brewery) and feature real log or coal fires in winter, flower-filled gardens for the summer (even in cities occasionally) and most importantly, thriving local custom. Many also offer characterful accommodation and restaurants serving high-quality fare. Pubs are prey to the same market forces as any other business, though, and many a delightful local has recently succumbed to exorbitant property prices or to the bland makeover favoured by the large chains. In 2012, pubs were closing at the rate of 12 a week due to the recession.

Essentials A-Z

Accident and emergency

For police, fire brigade, ambulance and, in certain areas, mountain rescue or coastguard, T999 or T112.

Disabled travellers

Wheelchair users, and blind or partially sighted people are automatically given 34-50% discount on train fares, and those with other disabilities are eligible for the **Disabled Person's Railcard**, which costs £20 per year and gives a third off most tickets. If you will need assistance at a railway station, call the train company that manages the station you're starting your journey from 24 hrs in advance. Disabled UK residents can apply to their local councils for a concessionary bus pass. **National Express** have a helpline for disabled passengers, T08717-818179, to plan journeys and arrange assistance. They also sell a discount coach card for £10 for people with disabilities.

The **English Tourist Board** website, www.visitengland.com, has information on the National Accessible Scheme (NAS) logos to help disabled travellers find the right accommodation for their needs, as well as details of walks that are possible with wheelchairs and the Shopmobility scheme. Many local tourist offices offer accessibility details for their area.

Useful organizations include:
Radar, T020-7250 3222, www.radar.org.uk. A good source of advice and information. It produces an annual National Key Scheme Guide and key for gaining access to over 9000 toilet facilities across the UK.
Tourism for all, T0845-124 9971, www. holidaycare.org.uk, www.tourismforall. org.uk. An excellent source of information about travel and for identifying accessible accommodation in the UK.

Electricity

The current in Britain is 240V AC. Plugs have 3 square pins and adapters are widely available.

Health

For minor accidents go to the nearest casualty department or an Accident and Emergency (A&E) Unit at a hospital. For other enquiries phone NHS Direct 24 hrs (T0845-4647) or visit an NHS walk-in centre. See also individual town and city directories throughout the book for details of local medical services.

Money → *For up-to-date exhange rates, see www.xe.com.*

The British currency is the pound sterling (£), divided into 100 pence (p). Coins come in denominations of 1p, 2p, 5p, 10p, 20p, 50p, £1 and £2. Banknotes come in denominations of £5, £10, £20 and £50. The last of these is not widely used and may be difficult to change.

Banks and bureaux de change

Banks tend to offer similar exchange rates and are usually the best places to change money and cheques. Outside banking hours you'll have to use a bureau de change, which can be easily found at the airports and train stations and in larger cities. **Thomas Cook** and other major travel agents also operate bureaux de change with reasonable rates. Avoid changing money or cheques in hotels, as the rates are usually poor. Main post offices and branches of **Marks and Spencer** will change cash without charging commission.

Credit cards and ATMs

Most hotels, shops and restaurants accept the major credit cards though some places may charge for using them. Some smaller establishments such as B&Bs may only accept cash.

Currency cards

If you don't want to carry lots of cash, prepaid currency cards allow you to preload money from your bank account, fixed at the day's exchange rate. They look like a credit or debit card and are issued by specialist money changing companies, such as Travelex and Caxton FX. You can top up and check your balance by phone, online and sometimes by text.

Money transfers

If you need money urgently, the quickest way to have it sent to you is to have it wired to the nearest bank via **Western Union**, T0800-833833, www.westernunion.co.uk, or **MoneyGram**, www.moneygram.com. The Post Office can also arrange a MoneyGram transfer. Charges are on a sliding scale; so it will cost proportionally less to wire out more money. Money can also be wired by **Thomas Cook**, www.thomasexchangeglobal. co.uk, or transferred via a bank draft, but this can take up to a week.

Taxes

Most goods are subject to a Value Added Tax (VAT) of 20%, with the major exception of food and books. VAT is usually already included in the advertised price of goods. Visitors from non-EU countries can save money through shopping at places that offer Tax Free Shopping (also known as the Retail Export Scheme), which allows a refund of VAT on goods that will be taken out of the country. Note that not all shops participate in the scheme and that VAT cannot be reclaimed on hotel bills or other services.

Cost of travelling

England can be an expensive place to visit, and London and the south in particular can eat heavily into your budget. There is budget accommodation available, however, and backpackers will be able to keep their costs down. Fuel is a major expense and won't just cost an arm and a leg but also the limbs of all remaining family members, and public transport – particularly rail travel if not booked in advance – can also be pricey, especially for families. Accommodation and restaurant prices also tend to be higher in more popular destinations and during the busy summer months.

The minimum daily budget required, if you're staying in hostels or camping, cycling or hitching (not recommended), and cooking your own meals, will be around £30 per person per day. If you start using public transport and eating out occasionally that will rise to around £35-40. Those staying in slightly more upmarket B&Bs or guesthouses, eating out every evening at pubs or modest restaurants and visiting tourist attractions can expect to pay around £60 per day. If you also want to hire a car and eat well, then costs will rise considerably to at least £75-80 per person per day. Single travellers will have to pay more than half the cost of a double room, and should budget on spending around 60-70% of what a couple would spend.

Opening hours

Businesses are usually open Mon-Sat 0900-1700. In towns and cities, as well as villages in holiday areas, many shops open on a Sun but they will open later and close earlier. For banks, see above. For TIC opening hours, see the tourist information sections in the relevant cities, towns and villages in the text.

Post

Most post offices are open Mon-Fri 0900 to 1730 and Sat 0900-1230 or 1300. Smaller sub-post offices are closed for an hour at lunch (1300-1400) and many of them operate out of a shop. Stamps can be bought at post offices, but also from many shops. A 1st-class letter weighing up to 100 g to anywhere in the UK costs 60p (a large letter over 240 mm by 165 mm is 90p) and should arrive the following day, while 2nd-class letters weighing up to 100 g cost 50p (69p) and take between 2-4 days. For more information about Royal Mail postal services, call T08457-740740, or visit www.royalmail.com.

Safety

Generally speaking, England is a safe place to visit. English cities have their fair share of crime, but much of it is drug-related and confined to the more deprived peripheral areas. Trust your instincts, and if in doubt, take a taxi.

Telephone → Country code +44.

Useful numbers: operator T100; international operator T155; directory enquiries T192; overseas directory enquiries T153.

Most public payphones are operated by **British Telecom** (BT) and can be found in towns and cities, though less so in rural areas. Numbers of public phone booths have declined in recent years due to the advent of the mobile phone, so don't rely on being able to find a payphone wherever you go. Calls from BT payphones cost a minimum of 60p, for which you get 30 mins for a local or national call. Calls to non-geographic numbers (eg 0845), mobile phones and others may cost more. Payphones (few and far between these days) take either coins (10p, 20p, 50p and £1), 50c, 1 or 2 euro coins, credit cards or BT Chargecards, which are available at newsagents and post offices displaying the BT logo. These cards come in denominations of £2, £3, £5 and £10. Some payphones also have facilities for internet, text messaging and emailing.

For most countries (including Europe, USA and Canada) calls are cheapest Mon-Fri between 1800 and 0800 and all day Sat-Sun. For Australia and New Zealand it's cheapest to call from 1430-1930 and from 2400-0700 every day. However, the cheapest ways to call abroad from England is not via a standard UK landline provider. Calls are free using **Skype** on the internet, or you can route calls from your phone through the internet with **JaJah** (www.jajah.com) or from a mobile using **Rebtel**. Many phone companies offer discounted call rates by calling their access number prior to dialling the number you want, including www. dialabroad.co.uk and www.simply-call.com.

Area codes are not needed if calling from within the same area. Any number prefixed by 0800 or 0500 is free to the caller; 08457 numbers are charged at local rates and 08705 numbers at the national rate.

Time

Greenwich Mean Time (GMT) is used from late Oct to late Mar, after which time the clocks go forward 1 hr to British Summer Time (BST).

Tipping

Tipping in England is at the customer's discretion. In a restaurant you should leave a tip of 10-15% if you are satisfied with the service. If the bill already includes a service charge, which is likely if you are in a large group, you needn't add a further tip. Tipping is not normal in pubs or bars. Taxi drivers may expect a tip for longer journeys, usually around 10%.

Tourist information

Tourist information centres (TICs) can be found in most towns. Their addresses, phone numbers and opening hours are listed in the relevant sections of this book. Opening hours vary depending on the time of year, and many of the smaller offices are closed or have limited opening hours during the winter months. All tourist offices provide information on accommodation, public transport, local attractions and restaurants, as well as selling books, local guides, maps and souvenirs. Many also have free street plans and leaflets describing local walks. They can also book accommodation for a small fee.

Museums, galleries and historic houses

Over 300 stately homes, gardens and countryside areas, are cared for by the **National Trust**, T0844-800 1895, www.nationaltrust.org.uk. If you're going to be visiting several sights during your stay, then it's worth taking annual membership, which costs £53, £25 if you're aged under 26 and £70 for a family, giving free access to all National Trust properties. A similar organization is **English Heritage**, T0870-333 1181, www.english-heritage.org.uk, which manages hundreds of ancient monuments and other sights around England, including Stonehenge, and focuses on restoration and preservation. Membership includes free admission to sites, and advance information on events, and costs £47 per adult to £82 per couple, under-19s free. **Natural England**, T0845-600 3078, www.naturalengland.org.uk, is concerned with restoring and conserving the English countryside, and can give information on walks and events in the countryside.

Many other historic buildings are owned by local authorities, and admission is cheap, or in many cases free. Most municipal **art galleries** and **museums** are free, as well as most state-owned museums, particularly those in London and other large cities. Most fee-paying attractions give a discount or concession for senior citizens, the unemployed, full-time students and children under 16 (those under 5 are admitted free in most places). Proof of age or status must be shown.

Finding out more

The best way of finding out more information is to contact Visit England (aka the English Tourist Board), www.visitengland.com. Alternatively, you can contact VisitBritain, the organization responsible for tourism. Both organizations can provide a wealth of free literature and information such as maps, city guides and accommodation brochures. Travellers with special needs should also contact VisitEngland or their nearest VisitBritain office. If you want more detailed information on a particular area, contact the specific tourist boards; see in the main text for details.

Visas and immigration

Visa regulations are subject to change, so it is essential to check with your local British embassy, high commission or consulate before leaving home. Citizens of all European countries – except Albania, Bosnia Herzegovina, Kosovo, Macedonia, Moldova, Turkey, Serbia and all former Soviet republics (other than the Baltic states) – require only a passport to enter Britain and can generally stay for up to 3 months. Citizens of Australia, Canada, New Zealand, South Africa or the USA can stay for up to 6 months, providing they have a return ticket and sufficient funds to cover their stay. Citizens of most other countries require a visa from the commission or consular office in the country of application.

The **UK Border Agency**, www.ukba.homeoffice.gov.uk, is responsible for UK immigration matters and its website is a good place to start for anyone hoping visit, work, study or emigrate to the UK. For visa extensions also contact the UK Border Agency via the website. Citizens of Australia, Canada, New Zealand, South Africa or the USA wishing to stay longer than 6 months will need an Entry Clearance Certificate from the British High Commission in their country. For more details, contact your nearest British embassy, consulate or high commission, or the Foreign and Commonwealth Office in London.

Weights and measures

Imperial and metric systems are both in use. Distances on roads are measured in miles and yards, drinks poured in pints and gills, but generally, the metric system is used elsewhere.

Contents

Oxford & around

Very much the capital of its county, England's oldest and most famous university town (once dubbed "the home of lost causes" by the poet Matthew Arnold) rarely disappoints. Arnold noted that, when seen from a distance, the city's spires, turrets and domes seem to be dreaming. Walking around the old stone colleges or through their surrounding meadows and gardens, it's impossible not to be aware of the weight of centuries of scholarship, culture and learning. Thankfully, though, the streets are as alive today as they've ever been. More urban and spacious than Cambridge, its equally celebrated sister in the east, Oxford continues to be one of the most remarkable, least isolated and most intellectually engaging of modern European cities.

To the west, the Thames comes wandering in over a wide and fertile plain, past Kelmscott, Buscot and medieval manor houses such as Stanton Harcourt. To the northwest, the Windrush Valley is dotted with exceptionally attractive stone villages like Minster Lovell, between the old market town of Witney and the honey-stone bustle of Burford, where the Cotswolds begin.

Oxford's name means many things to most people: above all though, it's still a university city of international standing. First-time visitors can hardly fail to be impressed by the sheer number of beautiful old colleges that make up this pinnacle of British academe. And it comes as some surprise that in the 21st century these mellow stone buildings, with their beamed halls, chapels, quads and spires, continue to be used pretty much for their original purpose. Christ Church is the grandest, Merton the oldest, New College the most authentic in its groundplan and Magdalen the loveliest, but all the colleges in the centre of the city are worth looking around. Unfortunately, they have an ambivalent attitude to opening their doors to casual observers, making access unpredictable (although most are open at some time in the afternoon). The colleges aside, there's so much else in the city to enjoy, not least two of the most extraordinary museums in the country: the Ashmolean and the Pitt Rivers. Views over the 'dreaming spires' can be had from several church towers in the middle of town. The Botanical Gardens are a delightful retreat on the riverside, next to flowering water meadows just beyond the old city walls. And then there's punting on the river, almost a mandatory activity in summer for students and visitors alike. If all the boats are booked up, simply taking a stroll in the green acres so close to the city centre makes for an exceedingly pleasant afternoon. As one of Europe's most remarkable cities, Oxford is, of course, mobbed in high season. That said, it's never too difficult to escape the crowds, and even the passing visitor is likely to appreciate the highly charged meeting of cerebral old institutions with bright young things.

Arriving in Oxford

Getting there Trains from London Paddington run very regularly and take between one and two hours; those via Reading usually have fewer stops than those going via Didcot Parkway. Oxford's one-way road system has reduced motorists to tears, and parking is almost impossible in the middle of the city without paying through the nose. However, there are several **Park & Ride** options. Thornhill Park and Ride, to the west, and Seacourt, to the east, are served by bus number 400 and tend to fill up very early in the day; bus 300 serves Pear Tree Park and Ride (to the north) and Redbridge (to the south). Water Eaton Park & Ride, a little further north, takes you into town by bus 500, and despite being further out, is often one of the quickest routes into the centre. If you must arrive on four wheels, you'll find Oxford just off the M40, about an hour from London, half an hour from the M25. Oxford is very well served by **coach** companies. ▸▸ *For further details, see Transport, page 38.*

Getting around **Walking** or **cycling** around central Oxford is one of life's real pleasures. For some of the slightly further-flung parts of the city, **taxis** are relatively cheap and the **bus** network from Gloucester Green along the High Street and around Carfax is regular and reliable. The centre of the city of Oxford is Carfax, the crossroads at the top of the High Street. Pedestrianized Cornmarket heads north from Carfax into wide St Giles, eventually leading to Woodstock and Banbury. High Street stretches east to Magdalen Bridge, while Queen Street continues west, down past the Norman Castle and prison towards the train station. St Aldate's slopes downhill south, past Christ Church College, with its prominent Tom Tower, crossing the Thames at Folly Bridge and continuing out of town as the Abingdon Road.

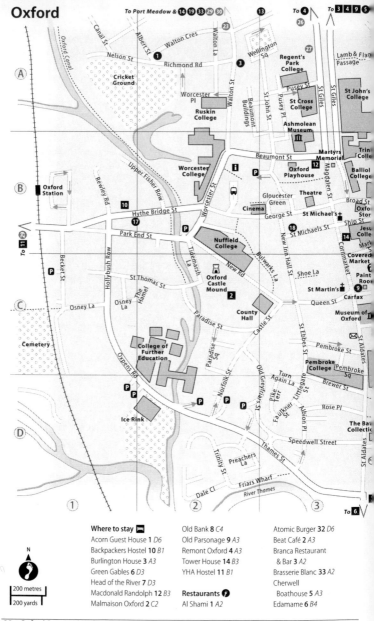

Oxford

To Port Meadow & **14 19 33 29 30**   **13**   To **4**   To **3 4 9 5**

Where to stay 🛏

Acorn Guest House **1** *D6*
Backpackers Hostel **10** *B1*
Burlington House **3** *A3*
Green Gables **6** *D3*
Head of the River **7** *D3*
Macdonald Randolph **12** *B3*
Malmaison Oxford **2** *C2*

Old Bank **8** *C4*
Old Parsonage **9** *A3*
Remont Oxford **4** *A3*
Tower House **14** *B3*
YHA Hostel **11** *B1*

Restaurants 🍴

Al Shami **1** *A2*

Atomic Burger **32** *D6*
Beat Café **2** *A3*
Branca Restaurant
 & Bar **3** *A2*
Brasserie Blanc **33** *A2*
Cherwell
 Boathouse **5** *A3*
Edamame **6** *B4*

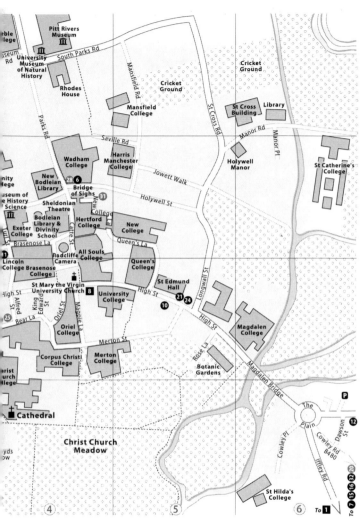

Gardeners Arms **4** *A3*	Missing Bean **11** *B4*	SoJo **17** *B1*	The House **22** *C4*
Gee's **8** *A3*	Moya **12** *D6*	Zappi's Bike Café **18** *B3*	King's Arms **28** *B4*
Golden Cross Pizza	Peppers Burgers **19** *A2*		Perch **29** *B1 or A2*
Express **9** *C3*	Pierre Victoire Bistrot **13** *A3*	**Pubs & bars** 🍺	Raoul's Bar **23** *A3*
Grand Café **10** *C5*	Quarter Horse Coffee **16** *D6*	Bear **25** *C4*	Trout Inn **30** *A2*
Jericho Café **14** *A2*	Queen's Lane	Café Tarifa **20** *D6*	Turf Tavern **31** *B4*
Kazbar **15** *D6*	Coffee House **21** *C5*	Duke of Cambridge **26** *A3*	
Malikas **7** *D6*	Rose **24** *C5*	Eagle & Child **27** *A3*	

Information The **TIC** ⓘ *15-16 Broad St, T01865-252200, www.visitoxfordandoxfordshire. com. Summer Mon-Sat 0930-1730, Sun 1000-1600, winter Mon-Sat 0930-1700, Sun 1000-1530,* provide an accommodation booking service.

History

Compared to many towns and cities in England, Oxford is not that old. There's no evidence of occupation in Roman times, although by then there was already a major road junction just to the north near Bicester. Even the Saxons probably only used the place as a river-crossing for their cattle, hence 'Oxenford', and never settled. In the late ninth century, though, King Alfred recognized the strategic importance of the gravelly banks at the confluence of the rivers Thames and Cherwell in defending his kingdom against the Danes. The town must have prospered, because the expected attack did come in 1009. The first Norman constable, Robert Doilly, built a castle overlooking the river in the west (of which one tower and the keep's mound survive) and ordered the construction of one of the first stone bridges in western Europe. **Folly Bridge**, completed in 1827, incorporating the Norman bridge beneath, is now a scheduled ancient monument. It wasn't until the late 12th century, when Henry II's wars with France prevented scholars from attending the University of Paris, that Oxford's position slap bang in the middle of England, well-connected to London and the rest of the country, made it a popular meeting place for informal gatherings of masters and wannabe masters. The South Range of Worcester College's main quad gives some idea of the houses these early academics favoured. Merton's Mob Quad is the oldest of the type of accommodation that they eventually adopted, although New College remains the most complete example of the hall, chapel and staircases later adopted by all colleges. The amazing Divinity School in the Bodleian Library was the first place to be owned by the university as a whole, before colleges were set up to safeguard the investments of benefactors. These religious foundations were dealt a hammer-blow by the Reformation but, thankfully, much of their architecture survived, making the city the best place in the country to explore Gothic and later neoclassical architecture. During the Civil War – which was fanned in part by the overhaul of the Church of England by Archbishop Laud of St John's College – Charles I based himself and his supporters at Christ Church. Come the Restoration, the university rose again, with illustrious alumni such as Christopher Wren (architect of the Sheldonian, Tom Tower and the Clarendon building) and the scientists Robert Boyle and Elias Ashmole. The 18th century was not a happy time in the university's history. Riddled with indolent Tories, it gained a reputation as as a marriage market for feckless aristos. The coming of the canal changed all that. The city expanded north, and today the spirit of Victorian Oxford and its industry can best be appreciated at the University Museum opposite the splendid red-brick confection of Keble College. In modern times, the Eagle Ironworks and Cowley car plant hugely increased the city's population. The suburbs in the north along the Banbury Road were for dons and their families, while Jericho was developed as affordable accommodation for artisans. East Oxford housed the workers in the car plant as it still just about does today.

West of Carfax

Most visitors using public transport approach central Oxford from the west. Walking up from the train station, the route up Hythe Bridge Street runs past the **Saïd Business School** (quite a sight in itself, with students perched at their terminals on display behind its glass front), over the Oxford Canal, and joins George Street at the junction of Worcester Street.

George Street continues gently uphill, past Gloucester Green bus station and market square on the left. The city meets the university proper 60 yards from the bus depot at the top of George Street where it hits Cornmarket. Most of the more interesting colleges are east of here, along Broad Street and the High Street (see East of Carfax, below).

One exception is **Worcester College**. A relatively young college, founded in 1714, its very grand 18th-century neoclassical buildings and lakeside garden surround the oldest example of scholars' accommodation in the city. The medieval South Range of the main quadrangle forms the adorably dinky remains of Gloucester College, a Benedictine monastery founded in 1283. Worcester Street heads north and becomes Walton Street, home to the **Ruskin Art School** (look out for degree shows by the most fashionable undergraduates at the university) and the Oxford University Press. The **Oxford University Press Museum** ① *Great Clarendon St, archives@oup.com, Mon-Fri 1000-1600 (not bank holidays) but book a time slot in advance, free*, has been recently refurbished. A little further down, between Walton Street and the canal, **Jericho** has long been one of the most happening parts of town (see Restaurants and Shopping below). At the top of Walton Street, Walton Well Road heads left down to **Port Meadow**, an amazingly unspoilt medieval watermeadow, still popular with skaters in winter, and frequented in the summer by grazing cows and undergraduates strolling over to pubs like the *Perch* and the *Trout* on the river.

A right turn eastwards at the meeting of Worcester Street and Walton Street leads on to Beaumont Street. Here stands the Oxford Playhouse, which is opposite the **Ashmolean Museum** ① *Beaumont St, T01865-278000, www.ashmolean.org, Tue-Sun and bank holiday Mon 1000-1800, but check the website for early closure days, free*, the oldest museum open to the public in the country. It was opened early in the 17th century by Elias Ashmole, one of Charles I's tax-men. Today it ranks as one of the most extraordinary collections under one roof outside London. The grand classical façade hides more than 60 rooms, displaying art and archaeology from ancient times to the present day. The museum was totally refurbished in 2009, and the displays and galleries are now arranged around the theme 'Crossing Cultures, Crossing Time'. The best place to start is on the ground floor, home to the Ancient World exhibit. These rooms are full of artefacts from ancient Egypt, including the Princesses fresco from about 1340 BC, a fragment of delicate wall painting; artefacts from ancient Cyprus and Greece; artefacts from Rome, and Italy before Rome; from India, and ancient Chinese paintings. The first floor, Asian Crossroads, shifts forward in time and displays the museum's collection of Indian and Islamic art, showing the connections between Asia and the Mediterranean via trading routes. Moving up to the second floor, the East Meets West gallery is an impressive and extensive display of art and musical instruments from the Western world and from Japan and China, and includes pieces from the Italian Renaissance. Up to the next floor where gallery 3M displays the museum's collection of art from 1800 to the present day – a fantastic collection, including a whole room of Pissarro. Also on the third floor is the Special Exhibitions gallery; see the website for what's currently on display. Down in the basement are new galleries on Exploring the Past, along with the museum shop and café. Connected to the museum after a 2010 refurbishment is the **Cast Gallery** accessible from the Rome gallery on the ground floor, with an exceptional array of around 900 casts taken from Greek and Roman sculptures in other collections around the world.

With the *Randolph Hotel* on the corner, Beaumont Street meets the wide, tree-lined north–south thoroughfare of St Giles at the spikey **Martyrs Memorial**. It was erected in 1841 in memory of the Protestant bishops Cranmer, Ridley and Latimer who were burned at the stake during the counter-Reformation of 'Bloody Mary' in the mid-16th century. A cross marks the exact spot where their ashes were found outside Balliol College on the Broad (see below). Over the way is **St John's College**, consistently one of the highest academic achievers, with one of the most beautiful gardens in Oxford, fronted by a striking combination of Gothic and neoclassical architecture.

East of Carfax

The block of old streets and colleges formed by the Cornmarket, the Broad, Catte Street and the High Street is pretty much the heart of the university, embracing the University Church of St Mary the Virgin, the Radcliffe Camera, the Bodleian Library and Sheldonian Theatre, as well as Jesus, Exeter and Brasenose colleges.

Cornmarket itself may not be the most inspiring street in the centre, but it conceals some hidden gems. The small **Painted Room** ① *3 Cornmarket (above Republic and hidden by an 18th-century façade)*, is where Shakespeare is supposed to have stayed when in town. The bard was apparently godfather to the son of the keeper of the Crown Inn that once stood on this site, John Davenant. Wooden panels on one wall slide back to reveal some remarkable Tudor wall painting, with white Canterbury bells, windflowers, roses and even a passion flower interlaced in the twisting design. The Oxford Preservation Trust are currently negotiating access with the owners, Oxford City Council, so access is limited, but contact the Trust on T01865-242918 for up-to-date information on visits. Behind is the **Covered Market**, now faintly twee but nonetheless another unusual survivor and an 18th-century precursor to modern shopping malls, currently occupied by some tempting permanent stalls. It's a great spot for buying picnic foods in the summer (see Shopping, page 37). On the way through from Cornmarket, more expansive but perhaps less significant medieval wall paintings can be seen behind glass on the walls of the local **Pizza Express**, re-named the **Golden Cross Restaurant** in honour of the inn that once stood here. At the top of the Cornmarket, the Saxon **tower of St Michael's** ① *T01865-255776, summer daily 1030-1700, winter daily 1030-1600*, at the North Gate, on the corner of Ship Street, was built in about 1040, allowing it to be dubbed the 'oldest building in Oxford', although the rest of the church is 13th century. The view from the top, reached via displays on the history of the church and some large bells, is definitely worth the climb.

A right turn at the end of Cornmarket heads into the Broad, perhaps the archetypical university street. Located here is **Balliol College**, not much to look at but one of the university's more radical powerhouses. Next door, **Trinity** has an unassuming cottage for a porter's lodge instead of the usual grand gatehouse, but the college's beauties include a late-17th-century chapel with carved limewood and juniper screen by Grinling Gibbons, and Wren's lovely Garden Quad, the first neoclassical building in the university.

Opposite Trinity, in the splendid late 17th-century building that once housed the Ashmolean, the **Museum of the History of Science** ① *Broad St, T01865-277280, www.mhs.ox.ac.uk, Tue-Fri 1200-1700, Sat 1000-1700, Sun 1400-1700, free*, displays a fascinating and old-fashioned collection of scientific landmarks: early chemical stills, chronometers, the original apparatus for manufacturing penicillin and Islamic and European astrolabes.

Next door, the **Sheldonian Theatre** ① *Broad St, T01865-277299, www.ox.ac.uk/sheldonian, Mar-Oct 1000-1230 and 1400-1630; Nov-Feb 1400-1530 (subject to university events), £2.50, concessions £1.50*, is the university's hall of ceremonies, also designed by Wren, who studied astronomy nearby at All Souls. Its ceiling is painted with the triumph of Truth, allied with Arts and Sciences, over Ignorance. An octagonal rooftop cupola above provides sheltered wraparound views of that famous skyline come wind or rain.

Its neighbour, the **Clarendon Building**, was constructed by Wren's pupil Hawksmoor to the plans of Vanbrugh, architect of Blenheim Palace, as a printing house. Now it makes a grand front door for the **Bodleian Library** ① *Broad St, T01865-277000, www.bodley. ox.ac.uk, Mon-Fri 0900-1700, Sat 0900-1630, Sun 1100-1700 (subject to university events); no children under 11; tours range from £2.50 to £13 and last from 30 to 90 mins; access to the Divinity School £1; first come, first serve on all tickets except the extended tour*, the university's chief academic resource and one of the greatest, certainly the oldest public libraries in the world. Its extraordinary Gothic Jacobean central courtyard has to be seen to be believed. Through the glass doors on the right, the 15th-century Divinity School is the oldest part of the building, with a magnificent vaulted stone ceiling, and served as the Infirmary in the Harry Potter films. The library itself is one of the wonders of the western world; its most ancient room, the mysterious and magical Duke Humfrey's Library was also used in the Harry Potter films, as Hogwarts library.

The library makes up the north side of Radcliffe Square, effectively the centre of the university, with 18th-century Scottish architect James Gibbs' majestic domed **Radcliffe Camera** plonked unceremoniously in the middle. Originally intended as a medical library, it now houses the English literature, film studies and history sections of the Bodleian library and is closed to the public. On the south side of the square, the **University Church of St Mary** seals the university off from the High Street behind. The church itself has a long history of ecclesiastical wrangling, but most visitors come for the climb up the **tower** ① *T01865-279111, Mon-Sat 0900-1700, Sun 1145-1700 (Jul, Aug until 1800), last admission 30 mins before closing, £4, children £3*, to overlook the Radcliffe Camera. It's probably the best viewpoint (and the highest) in the centre of the city. Round on the High Street side, the barley-sugar columns and broken pediment of the original church porch were possibly inspired by a Raphael cartoon in the collection of Charles I.

Nathaniel Hawthorne described the High Street as the "noblest old street in England", an impression confirmed now that it's virtually traffic-free apart from buses. It curves round to the south, with the postgraduate college **All Souls** (the 15th-century stained glass and oak roof of its chapel can be inspected on request) on the left, facing **University College**, not the oldest but certainly one of the most academic colleges. Next door, over Logic Lane, are the Victorian Examination Schools, still in use, opposite **Queen's College** which occupies flamboyant Baroque buildings. A left turn beyond leads up narrow Queens Lane, past the medieval **St Edmund Hall** into New College Lane, which is lined with famous gargoyles and twists around beneath the mock **'Bridge of Sighs'** back to the Broad. **New College** is famous for its chapel, hall and cloisters, and for its beautiful gardens, which are dominated by the old city wall and a viewing mound supposedly marking the site of a plague pit.

Back on the High Street, continuing south, the **Botanic Gardens** ① *T01865-286690, Nov-Feb 0900-1600, Mar/Apr and Sep/Oct 0900-1700, May-Aug 0900-1800, last entry 45 mins before close, £4.50, concessions £3, children free*, are on the right beyond Rose Lane, sheltering behind high walls and ornate Jacobean stone gates. The oldest of their kind in Britain (dating from 1621), they evolved from an apothecary's herb garden into this well-labelled horticultural wonderland, with tropical glasshouses, a walled garden and charming riverside walks. Rose Lane leads into **Christ Church meadow**, Oxford's answer to Cambridge's 'backs'.

Over the road, next to its bridge and beneath its unmistakable perpendicular tower, stands **Magdalen** (pronounced *Maudlin*) **College**, the most spread-out and gloriously sited of all the old colleges. The medieval chapel, hall and cloisters should be seen, but the highlight is the so-called New Building of 1733, an elegant neoclassical edifice standing in its very own deer park close by the confluence of the rivers Thames (or 'Isis' as it's called in Oxford) and Cherwell (pronounced *Char-wool*).

Southeast from here down **Cowley Road** is the pavement jewellery trail, a set of 58 ingots set into the pavement which form a puzzle which explains the history and evolution of this road.

North of Carfax

Museums and parks The wide green expanse of the **University Parks** to the north of the city centre are the destination of many a leisurely punt up from Magdalen Bridge or down from the Cherwell Boathouse. The parks also border a couple of museums. The **University Museum of Natural History** ① *Parks Rd, T01865-272950, www.oum.ox.ac.uk,* is unfortunately closed throughout 2013 for roof repairs, but check the website for details of how to see the collection via it's behind-the-scenes tours.

Just behind, the **Pitt Rivers Museum** ① *South Parks Rd, T01865-270927, www.prm.ox.ac. uk, Mon 1200-1630, Tue-Sun 1000-1630, free,* displays the university's anthropological and ethnographic collections in a famously fusty Victorian way: slide open draws to discover African charms and Inuit ornaments, and peer through glass cases at shrunken heads and Native American scalps. Children love it. Over the road from the museums, another Victorian marvel is the stripy red-brick and stone **Keble College**, where Holman Hunt's *Light of the World* in the chapel is the main attraction.

South of Carfax

Carfax Tower on the south side of the crossroads is all that remains of St Martin's Church, once the parish church of the city. The name Carfax derives from the Latin *quadri furcus* (four-forked), and indeed it was the church's position on such a busy crossroads that necessitated its demolition in 1896. The view south from **Carfax Tower** ① *daily 1000-1730, closes 1630 in Oct, £2.30, children £1.20,* is dominated by Wren's imposing gatehouse for Christ Church College, topped by Tom Tower.

Christ Church ① *T01865-276492, www.chch.ox.ac.uk, check the website for opening times and note that the college is often closed 1140-1430, last admission 1630, £7, children & concessions £5.50, family £14,* is the largest, most spectacular and most commercialized of the colleges. It was founded by Cardinal Wolsey (hence 'Cardinal College' in Hardy's *Jude the Obscure*) and re-founded by Henry VIII after his break with Rome; he saved some money by making its chapel the city's cathedral. The college is the university's largest and in Tom Quad you know it. Used by Royalists in the Civil War as a cattlepen, during the 18th century it became famous for the antics of its equally bovine aristocratic undergraduates or 'junior members' as they're known at 'the House'. Tom Quad, the cathedral and the picture gallery are well worth a look round. The **cathedral** ① *T01865-276155,* is the country's smallest and contains the recently restored shrine of the city's patron saint, St Frideswide, as well as some beautiful pre-Reformation stained glass, including an unusual depiction of the murder of St Thomas à Becket which survived because the martyr's head was replaced with plain glass. His face is still missing. Look out too for the illustration in the south transept of Osney Abbey, long since vanished. The **picture gallery** ① *accessed via Canterbury Gate, but you can enter from Oriel Sq if you are not in Christ Church, T01865-276172, Oct-May Mon, Wed & Sat 1030-1300 and 1400-1630, Sun 1400-1630, Jun Mon, Wed and Sat 1030-1700, Sun 1400-1700, Jul-Sep Mon-Sat 1030-1700, Sun 1400-1700, £3, concessions £2,* housed in a purpose-built modernist block sunk next to the library, is particularly famous for its collection of Old Master drawings.

These include the translucent beauty of Verrochio's *Head of a Young Woman* from the late 15th century, Bellini's *Portrait of a Man* and Leonardo's *Grotesque Head*, as well as works by Raphael, Durer, Titian, Rubens and Lorrain. The paintings on display include a 14th-century triptych, Tintoretto's *Portrait of a Gentleman*, Hals' *Portrait of a Woman* and Veronese's *Mystic Marriage of St Catherine*. One of the gallery's charms is the way that it has maintained intact the different tastes of its four major benefactors. As well as 13 future prime ministers, the Elizabethan soldier, courtier and poet Sir Philip Sydney, Robert Burton, author of *The Anatomy of Melancholy*, the poet and playwright Ben Jonson, art historian John Ruskin and archaeologist William Buckland, probably the college's most famous alumnus is Charles Lutteridge Dodgson, aka Lewis Carroll, the author of *Alice in Wonderland*. The garden gate behind the cathedral that supposedly inspired the mathematician's story has become something of a shrine.

Just up the hill from Christ Church on St Aldate's, the **Town Hall and Museum of Oxford** ① *St Aldate's, T01865-252351, Mon-Sat 1000-1700, Sun 1100-1500, free*, recently relocated into the town hall, gives the full low-down on the history of the city and its people with interactive activities for past and present. Off to the right down Pembroke Street, **Modern Art Oxford** ① *30 Pembroke St, T01865-722733, www.modernartoxford.org.uk, Tue and Wed 1000-1700, Thu-Sat 1000-1900, Sun 1200-1700, free*, is the city's top place for exhibitions of internationally respected contemporary art. A barn-like space, it's particularly suitable for large works and has a well-stocked bookshop attached.

Although the Thames actually enters Oxford from the north, its broad valley dominates the area west of the city. Meandering through open countryside, sometimes marred by pylons and reservoirs, the river gives this part of the country its special quality. The largest town, the old market centre of Witney, in fact straddles the River Windrush, one of the most charming of the Thames' tributaries. Descending from the Cotswold hills, the Windrush passes through the beautiful honey-coloured town of Burford, famously the 'gateway to the Cotswolds'. Then it winds through peaceful villages like Asthall, past the romantic ruined manor house at Minster Lovell, before finding the Thames just beyond Stanton Harcourt. Here a complete medieval estate is still inhabited by descendants of the Harcourt family. Further up the Thames, meanwhile, on opposite banks of the river, are two remarkable places associated with left-wing pioneers of very different types. The 16th-century manor house at Kelmscott was the delightful summer retreat of William Morris in late Victorian times, while the grey classical pile at Burcot witnessed the antics of some exotic Labour-leaning socialites and thinkers in the 1930s.

Getting there The A40 **road** heads west from north Oxford via Witney (10 miles) and Burford (17 miles) towards Cheltenham and Gloucester. It intersects with major roads running north–south at both Witney and Burford. **Stagecoach** ① *T01865-772250*, runs the S1 service from Oxford, which goes via Witney, and the S2, which goes to Witney and Minster Lovell. There are also buses to Burford. Other services link Lechlade with Cirencester and Swindon. ▸▸ *For further details, see Transport, page 38.*

Information Witney TIC ① *3 Welch Way, T01993-775802, daily 0900-1730.* **Burford TIC** ① *33a High St, T01993-823558, Mon-Sat 0930-1700, Sun 1000-1600.*

Upper Thames and Windrush valleys

The Thames runs south into Oxford. But going against the stream north and west out of the city, past Port Meadow, Godstow and some old abbey ruins, and heading west just south of the A40, the river skirts **Wytham Great Wood**. These 600 acres or so of deciduous hilltop woodland have been carefully managed by the university and now provide a habitat for all manner of rare north European birds, including nightingales, warblers and also a heronry. **Eynsham**, 3 miles west of the city ring road, was an important medieval town, a fact still reflected in its market square and old town hall. A mile south, at **Swinford**, the fine 18th-century bridge over the river operates the oldest and cheapest toll in the country. A couple more miles west, north of the Thames and east of the Windrush, **Stanton Harcourt** is a peaceful little grey-stone village. The surprisingly grand Norman cruciform church features one of the oldest screens in the country (13th-century) and a massive collection of monuments to the Harcourt family dating from the 12th century until the early 18th. Next door, their **manor house** ① *T01865-881928, Apr-Sep limited opening 1400-1800, please call for details*, was described by Alexander Pope as "the true picture of a genuine Ancient Country Seat," high praise from the greatest satirical poet of the Enlightenment, but then he was translating Homer's *Iliad* in the top of the tower here (open by appointment), in 1718. As well as 12 acres of gardens, complete with medieval fish and stew ponds, the old kitchen and private chapel are both very interesting.

Witney and around

Bypassed by the A40, the old market town of Witney has an attractive centre and splendid church. Just to its north, off the A4095, the **Cogges Manor Farm Museum** ① *Church Lane, T01993-772602, Farm Mar-Nov Tue-Sun 1100-1700, £4, children £3; manor house Sat, Sun and bank holidays, £5.50, children £4*, is worth the short detour. This attractive farmstead was reopened in 2011, showing small-scale and sustainable farming and how Cogges Farm has developed since Saxon times.

Three miles west of Witney, **Minster Lovell Hall and Dovecote** ① *(EH) usually Oct-Mar 1000-1600, free*, is a picturesque, ruined 15th-century manor house in a pleasant spot on the banks of the river Windrush, alongside an ancient dovecote.

Heading back towards the river, 6 miles south of Witney, **Bampton** is where Morris dancing is supposed to have originated, hence perhaps the unusually large number of pubs in the old town and also the unusually large number of men who enjoy them. The road south off the B4449 crosses the Thames at **Tadpole Bridge**, where there's a tiny campsite at Rushey Lock (not accessible by car) on one of the most unspoiled stretches of the river, and a pub, **The Trout Inn**.

Six miles west of Tadpole, **Kelmscott Manor** ① *T01367-252486, Apr-Oct Wed and Sat 1100-1700 (tickets available from 1030), £9, under-16s and students £4.50, garden only £2.50*, is a very fine 16th-century house hidden behind high walls in a quiet out-of-the-way village, where the great Socialist William Morris summered from 1871 until his death in 1896. He shared it with the pre-Raphaelite poet Gabriel Dante Rossetti. The place has been restored and preserved by the Society of Antiquaries as a home for a considerable collection of Morris's works – furniture, textiles and ceramics – in his highly influential, flowery (and usually poorly imitated) neo-medievalist style. Overall, a visit here confirms what Morris believed – that a great opportunity was lost during the industrial revolution to beautify the world with mass-production rather than cheapen it.

A walk west along the Thames Path from Kelmscott passes **Buscot Weir** and the National Trust village of Buscot, with its inevitable teashop; there are pleasant walks further along the river to the old Cheese Wharf. A mile or so east of Buscot village, **Buscot Park** ① *(NT), T01367-240786, www.buscot-park.com, Mar-Sep 1400-1800, check website for days, £8, children £4, grounds only £5*, was once famous as the weekend retreat of the left-wing thinkers, artists and poets that gathered around Gavin Henderson, Lord Faringdon, in the 1930s. An austere, late-18th-century house, it contains the Faringdon Collection, a particularly impressive art collection, including works by Rubens and Rembrandt and Burne-Jones's *Legend of the Briar Rose*, Sleeping Beauty to most of us. Upstairs, there are some remarkable English paintings of the 19th and 20th centuries by the likes of Gainsborough, Reynolds and Graham Sutherland. The spectacular Italianate water garden was laid out by Harold Peto in the early 20th century. On the way to it, the east pavilion is decorated with murals depicting the heady revolutionary fervour of the dinner parties held at the house.

Lechlade and around

Three miles northwest of Buscot, Lechlade on Thames (actually in a little pocket of Gloucestershire) is the highest navigable point on the river, and consequently a Mecca for pleasure cruisers. Best seen from the old St John's Bridge, next to yet another **Trout Inn** (see below), the spire of **St Lawrence's church** rises above the trees while the river snakes lazily across the meadows. The mainly 16th-century church inspired Shelley's *Stanzas in a Summer Evening Churchyard* on his boating trip up to Lechlade in 1815. The town itself comes as a bit of a disappointment, with its slightly desperate antique shops and poky little cafés, but nonetheless has a welcoming and friendly attitude, well-accustomed as it is to a stream of strangers messing about in boats.

Lechlade is also an important road junction. The A361 heads south from here for 10 miles to Swindon and north for 9 miles to Burford, crossing the A417 Wantage–Cirencester road. Five miles towards Burford, beyond a perfectly preserved 18th-century watermill at **Little Faringdon**, the **Swinford Museum** ① *Filkins, near Lechlade, T01367-860331, 1st Sun of May-Sep 1430-1700, free*, is one of the oldest small museums in Oxfordshire and contains a collection of domestic and agricultural tools housed in a 17th-century cottage.

Three miles further up the road to Burford, the **Cotswold Wildlife Park** ① *T01993-823006, www.cotswoldwildlifepark.co.uk, Apr-Oct daily 1000-1800 (last admission 1630), Nov-Mar daily 1000-1700 or dusk (last admission 1530), £14, children £9.50*, is set in acres of fine parkland around a Victorian manor house. It's a hugely popular local attraction where zebras and rhinos can be seen roaming their generous enclosures from the picnic lawns, while a miniature steam railway chugs around in the summer months. As well as caring for some endangered red pandas, the zoo also takes its gardening seriously, with a tropical house, 'hot bed' and walled garden.

Burford

Since its decline as an important medieval wool town, Burford has long billed itself as the 'Gateway to the Cotswolds' and strikingly lovely and stone-built it is too. That's no secret though, which means that during the summer months the gate pressure can be intense: the long broad High Street, sloping down to the old bridge over the little river Windrush, becomes impossibly busy. Even so, the crush in the antique shops, pubs and tearooms can easily be avoided on the smaller side streets. One such, at the lower end of the High Street, leads to Burford's **church of St John**, the most outstanding parish church in the county. Its Norman tower has survived, later topped with a spire, and the medieval warren of arches, chapels, nooks and crannies inside should definitely not be missed. The church has some intriguing monuments, including one to Henry VIII's hairdresser that features the first known depiction of a native South American in England. Another carving is a possible likeness of a fertility goddess from the second century. The font bears the scratched name of one of the mutinous Levellers imprisoned here by Oliver Cromwell for three nights in 1649. On 17 May, three of them were executed, an event still commemorated in the town on the nearest Saturday to that date with some fancy dress and not-so-fancy politicizing.

The town itself has retained, virtually unaltered, its medieval street plan. Originally, the main road ran east–west past the 16th-century market hall, called the **Tolsey** (now housing a local history museum); there are still several houses around it that bear traces of the Middle Ages. From the bridge, a very pleasant walk follows the banks of the Windrush eastwards for about three miles to the village of **Swinbrook**, where there's another church with remarkable tombs inside and the graves of Nancy and Unity Mitford outside.

Half a mile away to the north, at **Widford** is a tiny church in an even more idyllic setting and incorporating the remains of a Roman villa. The pretty and relatively undiscovered village of **Asthall**, a mile further downstream, is also well worth a visit. Another riverside walk heads west along the Windrush to **Taynton**, and a couple of miles further to **Great Barrington**, where The Fox Inn does excellent lunches and has accommodation (see below).

Oxford and around listings

For hotel and restaurant price codes and other relevant information, see pages 10-13.

⊖ Where to stay

Oxford *p21, map p22*

Hotels in Oxford are generally expensive for what you get, and hotels in the lower price brackets are almost non-existent although there are lots of B&Bs on Abingdon Rd and Banbury Rd. There are hardly enough affordable rooms for students in the city, so visitor accommodation is at a premium and you should book well in advance, especially in the summer. The TIC runs the usual booking service, but don't expect to be within walking distance of the sights if you leave it too late.

If you are visiting during university holidays, a great budget option is to stay in one of the colleges, from £30 a night B&B. Check www.oxfordrooms.co.uk to see what is available.

££££ The Macdonald Randolph, Beaumont St, T01865-256400, www. macdonaldhotels.co.uk. Landmark building in the city centre, home to the **Morse Bar** – recognizable as the bar of choice for Inspector Morse in the TV series.

££££ Malmaison Oxford, Oxford Castle, 3 New Rd, T0844-693 0659, www. malmaison.com. A former prison that is now a boutique hotel. It's rooms that are the real pull of this hotel: luxurious and original.

££££ Old Parsonage Hotel, 1 Banbury Rd, T01865-310210, www.oldparsonage-hotel. co.uk. Formerly Oscar Wilde's undergraduate digs and now one of the poshest hotels in town, run by the same people as **Gee's Restaurant**. Building dates back to 1660. Complimentary walking tours and bicycles available to guests.

£££ The Burlington House, 374 Banbury Rd, T01865-513513, www.burlington-hotel-oxford.co.uk. Charming and welcoming little boutique B&B some distance up the

Banbury Rd, but there are plenty of buses. Very good breakfast.

£££ Head of the River, Folly Bridge, St Aldate's, T01865-721600, www.headof theriveroxford.co.uk. Large Fuller's pub and hotel overlooking river to the south. Breakfast included.

£££ Old Bank Hotel, 92-94 High St, T01865-799599, www.oldbank-hotel.co.uk. One of the most stylish and central places to stay in the city. 42 individual rooms (likely to have good views of the famous skyline) and the **Quod Bar and Grill**, a stylish brasserie-type place with a sunny outdoor drinking deck in summer. Also offers free walking tours and bicycles to guests.

£££ Remont Oxford, 367 Banbury Rd, T01865-311020, www.remont-oxford.co.uk. Again, a little further away from the centre but easy to get the bus into town. This B&B has recently been refurbished to a hotel standard and is clean, spacious and chic.

£££-££ The Tower House, 15 Ship St, T01865-246828, www.oxfordhotelsand inns.com. Bang in the middle of town, in a 17th-century house, tucked away off Cornmarket, with 7 rooms.

££ Acorn Guest House, 260 Iffley Rd, T01865-247998, www.oxford-acorn.co.uk. Four comfortable double rooms, a 20-min walk into town. Similar in price and style to many of the B&Bs strung out along the main road into town from the south and east.

££ Green Gables Guest House, 326 Abingdon Rd, T01865-725870, www.green gables.uk.com. Offers 7 double rooms, fairly clean and comfortable, with breakfast; some way out town near Donnington Bridge.

£ The Backpackers Hostel, 9a Hythe Bridge St, T01865-721761, www.hostels.co.uk. Close to the station, and has 10 bunkrooms for 4-10 people each. Open 24 hrs.

£ YHA Hostel, 2a Botley Rd, T0845-371 9131. Just behind the railway station, this hostel can be reached from the westbound platform through a little alleyway. It is fairly smart with 180 beds in dorms and rooms. Open 24 hrs.

Camping
The Camping and Caravanning Club, 426 Abingdon Rd, on the ring-road south of Oxford, 1.5 miles from city centre. T0845-130 7633. Open all year, 129 sites.

West of Oxford *p30*
££££ Burford House Hotel, 99 High St, Burford, T01993-823151, www.burford-house.co.uk. In a stunning 17th-century building, this family-run hotel has plenty of friendly touches and a pleasant easy-going atmosphere.

££££ The Lamb, Sheep St, Burford, T01993-823155, www.cotswold-inns-hotels.co.uk. The former home of Sir Lawrence Tanfield, Lord Chief Baron of the Exchequer in the reign of Queen Elizabeth I, offers log fires, flagstone floors and real ales. Rooms are quiet and individually furnished in a comforting style. The fairly expensive restaurant does top-notch food, and there are sandwiches and deli boards at the bar.

££££ Old Swan & Minster Mill, Minster Lovell, T01993-774441, www.oldswanandminstermill.com. There are historical rooms and a gastro-pub in the Old Swan, with more modern (and modest) rooms next door in Minster Mill. Dog-friendly, for an extra charge.

£££ The Angel at Burford, Witney St, Burford, T01993-822714, www.theangelatburford.co.uk. A very highly rated pub-restaurant offering a gastro-pub style menu and spacious yet cosy double rooms.

£££ Bay Tree Hotel Sheep St, Burford, T01993-822791, www.cotswold-inns-hotels.co.uk. Wysteria-clad on the outside, chintzy within. Very comfortable, with a reputable restaurant.

£££ The Fox Inn, Great Barrington, near Burford, T01451-844385, www.foxinnbarrington.com. A very good pint can be had in this charming riverside pub with a garden. There's some very decent English

country cooking 7 days a week and 3 rooms with bathroom en suite.

££ The Ferryman Inn, Bablock Hythe, Northmoor, T01865-880028, www.theferrymaninn.co.uk. Closed Tue. A couple of miles from Stanton Harcourt, this famous waterside freehouse offers a ferry service across the river, simple but well-equipped rooms, pub grub and a very cheery atmosphere.

££ Rectory Farm, Northmoor, nr Witney, T01865-300207, www.oxtowns.co.uk/rectoryfarm. 2 B&B rooms are available in a very fine early 17th-century stone farmhouse that once belonged to St John's College, Oxford. Self-catering holiday cottages also available.

❼ Restaurants

Oxford *p21, map p22*
A lot of Oxford's trendy bars, cafés and restaurants rated by the locals are found off the Cowley Rd; the pricier establishments can be found in the centre of town. The other option for food as well as booze is one of the pubs (see below), even though they can sometimes become too lively to make eating a pleasure.

£££ Gee's Restaurant and Bar, 61 Banbury Rd, T01865-553540, www.gees-restaurant.co.uk. Enjoy your lunch in the newly renovated iconic glasshouse, originally used for growing vegetables in the 1890s.

£££-££ Brasserie Blanc, 71-72 Walton St, T01865-510999, www.brasserieblanc.com. Brasserie-style dishes at Raymond Blanc's chain; many think it's not particularly good value for money – the set menu is a better bang for your buck.

££ Branca Restaurant & Bar, 111 Walton St, T01865-556111, www.branca.co.uk. Popular, modern Italian restaurant, with a traditional menu, often very busy with a lively atmosphere.

££ The Cherwell Boathouse, Bardwell Rd, T01865-552746, www.cherwellboathouse.co.uk. Have a fine lunchtime feast in a clapperboard hut, then hire a punt. Or enjoy a more expensive and leisurely supper on the waterside.

££ Edamame, 15 Holywell St, T01865-246916, www.edamame.co.uk. Highly rated Japanese restaurant serving authentic dishes. No reservations, but worth the wait if there is a queue (there often is). Open for lunch Wed-Sun; for sushi on Thu evenings and also open for evening dining on Fri and Sat.

££ Golden Cross Pizza Express, Golden Cross Inn, off the Cornmarket, T01865-790442, www.pizzaexpress.com. Heavily restored in 1988 (see page 26). A good fall-back.

££ Moya, 97 St Clements St, T01865-200111, www.moya-oxford.biz. Traditional Slovak food with generous portions. Also serves as a cocktail bar.

££ Pierre Victoire Bistrot, 9 Little Clarendon St, T01865-316616, www.pierrevictoire.co.uk. Vibrant French bistro serving traditional food to expectant diners.

££-£ Al-Shami, 25 Walton Cres, T01865-310066, www.al-shami.co.uk. This restaurant has now been here 25 years and offers some superior Lebanese cuisine, with a particularly good mezze selection.

£ Atomic Burger, 96 Cowley Rd, T01865-790855, www.atomicburger.co.uk. May not have the best burgers in the world but does have a great, unusual menu, and the retro comic-book theme is fun.

£ The Gardeners Arms, 39 Plantation Rd, T01865-559814, www.thegarden-oxford.co.uk. Hearty vegetarian food.

£ Kazbar, 25-27 Cowley Rd, T01865-202920, www.kazbar.co.uk. Spanish and North African restaurant offering tasty tapas.

£ Malikas, 218 Cowley Rd, T01865-723029, www.malikasrestaurant.co.uk. An excellent contemporary Indian restaurant with a modern dining room.

£ Peppers Burgers, 84 Walton St, T01865-511592, www.peppersburgers.com. The pure beef burgers have been a hit with students for the last 25 years. Some say the best takeaway burger in Oxford is to be found here. Also does pizza.

£ SoJo, 6-9 Hythe Bridge St, T01865-202888, www.sojooxford.co.uk. Down by the station, no-frills, authentic Chinese food. Very highly rated by the locals.

Cafés

Grand Café, 84 High St, T01865-204463. Claims to be the oldest coffeehouse in England. Charming service and high prices for some superb cafetière coffees, American-style sandwiches and light meals.

Jericho Café, 112 Walton St, T01865-310840. A popular haunt for brunch.

The Missing Bean, Turl St, T01865-794886. Locally roasted Brazilian coffee, good ciabatta sarnies and a wide selection of home-baked cakes and pastries.

Quarter Horse Coffee, Cowley Rd, T01865-428808. Great coffee and great teas.

Queen's Lane Coffee House, 40 High St, T01865-240082. Also claiming to be the oldest coffeehouse in town, this place has been serving since 1654. Turkish coffee available, plus an extensive lunch menu.

The Rose, 51 High St, T01865-244429. A bright, refurbished little café with an imaginative menu and lovely afternoon teas.

Zappi's Bike Café, 28-32 St Michaels St, www.zappisbikecafe.com. A really friendly venue that serves up good coffee and home-made cakes.

West of Oxford *p30*
See also Where to stay, above, and Pubs, bars and clubs, below.

£££ The Trout Inn, Tadpole Bridge, Lechlade on Thames, T01367-252313, www.trout-inn.co.uk. This busy waterside oasis does good food and also has rooms available (**£££**).

££ Mermaid Inn, High St, Burford, T01993-822193, www.themermaidburford.co.uk. A very old building, with decent-enough pub grub.

££ The Royal Oak, Ramsden, near Witney, T01993-868213, www.royaloakramsden.com.

A freehouse that does very good food. Ramsden is a quiet village located on Akeman St, the Roman road that connected Bicester and Cirencester.

££ The Swan Inn, Swinbrook, T01993-823339, www.theswanswinbrook.co.uk, near the Windrush. A very old pub, where the food's all home-made and locally sourced, and the ales are well-kept.

Cafés
£ The Priory Tearoom, High St, Burford, T01993-823249. Good breakfasts and afternoon teas.

⚙ Pubs, bars and clubs

Oxford *p21, map p22*
Oxonians are understandably proud of the city's pubs.
The Bear, 6 Alfred St, T01865-728264, www.bearoxford.co.uk. A cosy, wood-panelled old pub popular with the local Christ Church students and also with rugby union clubs from around the world, judging by the array of old ties in the back bar. Not for tall people (ie anyone over 5ft 5). Good for cask ales.
Café Tarifa, Cowley Rd, T01865-256091, www.cafe-tarifa.co.uk. A relaxed cocktail bar with a Mediterranean/North African vibe and live music.
Duke of Cambridge, 5-6 Little Clarendon St, T01865-558173, www.dukebar.com. A popular and lively cocktail bar.
Eagle and Child, St Giles, T01865-302925, www.nicholsonspubs.co.uk. Known as the 'Bird and Baby', this is another cosy place to drink. It was once the favourite haunt of 'the Inklings', JRR Tolkien and CS Lewis.
The House, Blue Boar St, T01865-724433, www.housebar.co.uk. Buzzing cocktail bar with a great terrace and a games room.
King's Arms, on the corner of Holywell St and Broad St, T01865-242369, www.youngs.co.uk. Some good Young's beer but quite expensive grub. Popular with students.
The Perch, Binsey, T01865-728891, www.the-perch.co.uk, Wed-Sun only.

A little out of town but makes for a pleasant walk across Port Meadow and has a tree-shaded riverside garden.
Raoul's Bar, 32 Walton St, T01865-553732, www.raoulsbar.co.uk. Cocktail bar with an impressive menu.
The Trout Inn, Lower Wolvercote, T01865-510930, www.thetroutoxford.co.uk. Beside an old bridge and weir.
Turf Tavern, beyond Bath Pl off Holywell La. Yet another real ale pub, with reasonable pub grub served up all day to heaving crowds outside, beneath the old city wall of New College, and inside in the snug, low-ceilinged bars.

Clubs
Surprisingly short on good nightspots, Oxford's clubs come and go.
The Bridge, 6-9 Hythe Bridge St, T01865-242526, www.bridgeoxford.co.uk. Student nights in the week, but the club is over-21s only on Sat.
Lava & Ignite, Cantay House, Park End St, T01865-250181, www.lavaignite.com/oxford. A large venue with a spectrum of pop, dance and R'n'B.
Roppongi, 29 George St, T01865-241574, www.roppongioxford.com. One of the latest uber-cool offerings, marketing itself as chic, upmarket and elite.

West of Oxford *p30*
See also Where to stay and Restaurants, above.
The Bell, Ducklington, near Witney, T01993-702514, www.thebellinnducklington.co.uk. A thatched pub that has lovely flowers outside and traditional pub games, such as 'Aunt Sally', inside.
The Plough Inn, Kelmscott, T01367-253543, www.theploughinnkelmscott.com. A gorgeous little village pub with a wide selection of real ales.
White Hart Inn, Wytham, near the River Thames and the A34, T01865-244372, www.whitehartwytham.co.uk. Heated barn for winter surrounded by flowerbeds, situated on a quiet backroad.

✪ Entertainment

Oxford *p21, map p22*
Cinemas
Odeon, Magdalen St and **Odeon**, George St, T0871-224 4007, are the mainstream screens in the centre of town. The **Phoenix**, Walton St, T01865-512526, www.picturehouses. co.uk, shows mainstream and arthouse films and is inevitably a much nicer experience. The **Ultimate Picture Palace**, Jeune St, Cowley Rd, T01865-245288, www. uppcinema.co.uk, is a lovely independent cinema that shows arthouse, mainstream and classic movies.

Theatre and comedy venues
Burton Taylor Studio. Part of the Oxford Playhouse (see below), just next door. For innovative, new and fringe productions.
The Glee Club, Hythe Bridge St, T0871-472 0400, www.glee.co.uk/oxford. Comedy club and music venue, Fri and Sat.
New Theatre Oxford, George St, T01865-320760. Large-scale touring productions, musicals, operas and pantomimes.
Oxford Playhouse, Beaumont St, T01865-305305, www.oxfordplayhouse.com. The main theatre for drama and middle-scale touring productions by the likes of the National Theatre and Almeida Theatre Company.

✪ Shopping

Oxford *p21, map p22*
High St is a haven for independent shops and boutiques, including **Sanders of Oxford**, at No.104, a fascinating shop selling maps and fine prints; **Aspire**, which has an gorgeous collection of accessories, jewellery and gifts, and the **University of Oxford Shop**, at No.106, which does all those monogrammed sweatshirts and souvenirs to show the folks back home. Little Clarendon St is the place for gift shops and funky home furnishings, while Broad St is the place to go for bookshops and

art galleries. The **Old Fire Station Shop**, 40 George St, is a treasure trove of wares created by local artists and designers.

Books
Blackwell's, 48-51 Broad St, T01865-792792. The University booksellers, with an excellent second-hand section as well as all the latest new and academic titles.
Waterfield's, 52 High St, T01865-721809. An interesting second-hand and antiquarian bookseller.
Waterstone's, Broad St, T01865-790212.

Markets
For picnic materials, the **Covered Market** is home to: **Ben's Cookies**, T01865-247407, for huge, gooey delicious cookies in a variety of flavours; **Cake Shop** for cakes, biscuits and sweet decorations as well as doughs, and **Pieminister** for delicious pies made with quality ingredients.

✪ What to do

Oxford *p21, map p22*
Boating
Punts can be hired from **Cherwell Boathouse**, off Bardwell Rd, T01865-515978; **Magdalen Bridge Boat House**, Magdalen Bridge, T01865-202643, and **Salter's Steamers**, Folly Bridge, T01865-243421, www.salterssteamers.co.uk, who also run boat trips on the Thames. **College Cruisers**, Combe Rd Wharf, Combe Rd, T01865-554343, www.collegecruisers.com, hire out cruising boats on the river by the week.

Walking
Official guided tours leave from the TIC, where there are also some good self-guiding leaflets available on walks along the river or canal and around the town. The Oxford Canal walk runs all the way up to Coventry, on level ground, through picturesque countryside. The **Thames Path** can also be joined here (see page 31).

West of Oxford *p30*
Boating
Cotswold Boat Hire, The Trout Inn, St John's Bridge, Farringdon Rd, Lechlade on Thames, T01793-727083, same-day enquiries T07947-993784 (mob). Rowing boats, electric boats and day cruisers.

Riverside (Lechlade) Ltd, Park End Wharf, Lechlade, T01367-253599, www.riverside-lechlade.co.uk. For rowing boat, motor boat and cruiser hire.

⊖ Transport

Oxford *p21, map p22*
Bicycle
Oxford is great for cyclists. You can hire a bike for a day, week or month from **Walton St Cycles**, 78 Walton St, T01865-311610.

Bus
Long distance The intercity and local bus terminus is at Gloucester Green, very close to the city centre. **National Express**, T08717-818178, www.nationalexpress.com, for **London Victoria** and long distance. Also the **Oxford Tube**, T01865-772250 (24-hr London–Oxford express service).

Local Most local buses, including services to **Witney**, **Minster Lovell** and **Burford**, are run by **Stagecoach Oxford**, T01865-772250.

Car
Car hire Thrifty, Osney Mead, T01865-250252; **Oxford Hatchback Hire**, Longcot, Shotover Kilns, Old Rd,
Headington, T01865-763615; **Midlands Vehicle Rental Ltd**, www.mvrltd.co.uk.

Car parks Central car parks (many of which have hefty overnight charges) include Gloucester Green, Westgate, Worcester St, Abbey Pl and Oxpens Rd. Park and Ride is run by **Oxford Bus Co**, T01865-785400. Day return bus fare £1.50.

Taxi
Relatively cheap in Oxford, and it's not usually a problem finding one on the street. Otherwise **City Taxis** T01865-201201; 24-hr minicabs from **001 Taxis** T01865-240000.

Train
The main railway station is in the west of the city, where the Botley Rd meets Hythe Bridge St, a 15-min walk from the centre. Trains are run by **First Great Western** T0845-700 0125, www.firstgreat western.co.uk, and **Virgin Trains**, T0871-9774222, www.virgintrains.co.uk.

West of Oxford *p30*
Taxi
A to B Taxis, Kerrieview, Burford Rd, Minster Lovell, T01993-706060; **Fairways Airport & Tour Cars**, Burford, T01993-823152.

❶ Directory

Oxford *p21, map p22*
Hospitals John Radcliffe Hospital, Headley Way, Headington, T01865-741166, is the nearest casualty department.

Contents

North of the Cotswolds

Temptingly located just beyond the northern edge of the Cotswolds is the verdant Vale of Evesham, where the River Avon is the life-blood of the orchards and fields of fresh British produce. Evesham itself is the heart of this area, a bustling community centred around the river and the Abbey. It's an enchanting place to spend the day boating, especially in spring when the surrounding orchards are in full bloom.

Just to the northeast, within easy striking distance of Chipping Campden and Moreton-in-Marsh, is Stratford-upon-Avon, birthplace of the Bard and epicentre of Shakespeare Country. One of the most visited destinations in the whole of England, Stratford manages, surprisingly enough, to sustain the atmosphere of an ordinary Midland market town amid all the tourist trappings. Visitors can enjoy the fantastic historic architecture, which is preserved and utilized in the form of hotels, restaurants and attractions. What's more, this is no staid town stagnating in its own history – the Royal Shakespeare Theatre is the cultural heart of Stratford and draws audiences of all ages and tastes to its high-calibre productions.

Stratford-upon-Avon → *For listings, see pages 45-48.*

As the world centre of an ever-expanding Shakespeare industry and Britain's second-most visited tourist destination after London, you would naturally expect there to be a preponderance of bard-related attractions in and around Stratford, but the place has nevertheless still managed to hold onto its authentic market-town atmosphere. The Royal Shakespeare Company is one of the artistic triumphs of the United Kingdom, and no visit to Stratford is really complete without seeing some of Shakespeare's drama – the play really is the thing in comparison with the Birthplace Trust Shakespeare trail. But if you haven't got enough time, and you still want to do the 'Willgrimage', you might drop in on Shakespeare's birthplace which has a tolerable exhibition, or see where Shakespeare was buried in Holy Trinity Church. As for the locals, they live in peace with the bard's sometimes troublesome legacy.

Arriving in Stratford-upon-Avon
Getting there As far as **trains** are concerned, there's an embarrassment of riches including a steam service, the **Shakespeare Express** ① *T0121-707 4696, www.shakespeareexpress. com, Jul-Sep Sun only*, which runs from Birmingham's Snow Hill station. **Chiltern Railways** go from London and Birmingham regularly and offer discounts for flexible travel in the region with the 'Shakespeare Explorer' ticket.

The M40 provides a speedy driving route for those coming from the north or south. Simply take exit 15 onto the A46, where Stratford is clearly signposted. If you prefer a more picturesque route from the south, there's the A3400 from Oxford, which will take you straight into Stratford town centre via some delightful Cotswolds towns like Shipston on Stour (see below). From the southwest and the M5, take exit 9 at Tewkesbury and the A46 to Evesham (see below), then follow the signposts to Stratford. There's plenty of parking in Stratford.

Getting around Open-top sightseeing buses link Shakespeare's Birthplace, Anne Hathaway's Cottage and Hall's Croft and depart from the Visitor Information Centre on Bridgefoot.

Information The official **Visitor Information Centre** ① *Bridgefoot, T01789-264293, Mar-Oct daily 0900-1730, Nov-Feb Mon-Sat 0900-1730, Sun 1000-1600*, is by the Bridgefoot car park on one of the main routes in to Stratford-upon-Avon. This new, larger visitor centre has expanded to offer tickets, information, accommodation booking, internet and Skype services and a café.

Places in Stratford-upon-Avon
From the tourist office and Art Gallery see above, it's very easy to get to Stratford's main raison d'être: the **Royal Shakespeare Theatre**, towering over the landscape like an art deco power station. In fact it's quite a complex set of buildings, carefully designed to serve the great god Thespus with a varied platter. Also nestling within the arms of this great beast is a more delicate flower, the **Swan Theatre**, which now shares its front-of-house space with the Royal Shakespeare Theatre.

As befits such a dramatic place, the theatre has a chequered history including fire, passion and suicide. The present building was designed by Elizabeth Scott and was opened in 1932, but the original theatre on this site dates back to 1879 when a local brewer Edward Flower donated the land for the building. For a fascinating view behind the scenes, take a **theatre tour** ① *T0844-800 1110, www.rsc.org.uk*; visit the RSC's **free exhibitions**, or

Stratford-upon-Avon

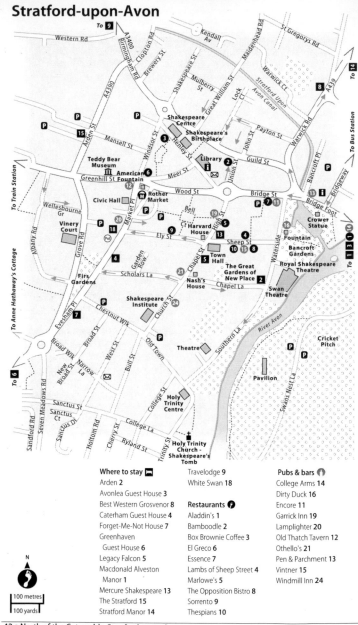

Where to stay 🛏
Arden **2**
Avonlea Guest House **3**
Best Western Grosvenor **8**
Caterham Guest House **4**
Forget-Me-Not House **7**
Greenhaven
  Guest House **6**
Legacy Falcon **5**
Macdonald Alveston
  Manor **1**
Mercure Shakespeare **13**
The Stratford **15**
Stratford Manor **14**

Travelodge **9**
White Swan **18**

Restaurants 🍴
Aladdin's **1**
Bamboodle **2**
Box Brownie Coffee **3**
El Greco **6**
Essence **7**
Lambs of Sheep Street **4**
Marlowe's **5**
The Opposition Bistro **8**
Sorrento **9**
Thespians **10**

Pubs & bars 🍺
College Arms **14**
Dirty Duck **16**
Encore **11**
Garrick Inn **19**
Lamplighter **20**
Old Thatch Tavern **12**
Othello's **21**
Pen & Parchment **13**
Vintner **15**
Windmill Inn **24**

climb the **Theatre Tower** ① *daily 1000-1600, £2.50, children £1.25*. Over 400 members of staff make scenery and costumes, maintain the theatre and administer its business.

Your most likely next port of call will be the collection of buildings run by the **Shakespeare's Birthplace Trust** ① *The Shakespeare Centre, Henley St, T01789-204016, www.shakespeare.org.uk, ticket for 5 properties £21.50, children £13.50, concessions £19.50, family £56 (valid for 1 year); other tickets also available*. The Shakespeare Centre is easily the most informative of the properties. There is a quite formidable team of Shakespeare scholars working with the Birthplace Trust, and a reading room which draws academics from round the world to look at this unique collection of first editions, history and scholarship. The centre can genuinely claim to be a site of world heritage. **Shakespeare's Birthplace** ① *Nov-Mar daily 1000-1600, Apr-Oct daily 1000-1700 (Jul and Aug until 1800)*, also on Henley Street, is the jewel in the crown of the Shakespeare Properties. Even if there are a few gaps in our knowledge of Will's life (just who was the Dark Lady?), the Birthplace Trust are determined to do Will proud with this shrine to the man and the place that shaped his early life. A five-minute walk away on Chapel Lane is **Nash's House & New Place** ① *Nov-Mar daily 1100-1600, Apr-Oct daily 1000-1700*, a well-preserved Tudor House that was home to Shakespeare's granddaughter, and the site of Shakespeare's final home, which has been excavated; its archaeological treasures are on show. Another five-minute walk to Old Town takes you to **Hall's Croft** ① *Nov-Mar daily 1000-1600, Apr-Oct daily 1000-1700*, the elegant Jacobean home of Shakespeare's daughter, Susanna, which display the intriguing apothecary equipment of her husband, a doctor. 2013 is the 400th anniversary of this property. Two miles west of the town is **Anne Hathaway's Cottage** ① *Shottery, Nov-Mar daily 1000-1600, Apr-Oct daily 0900-1700*, easily reached by car or a pleasant 30-minute walk. This is the second-most visited of the Shakespeare Properties and really is exquisitely maintained, with original furniture and the most beautiful gardens. Finally, three miles north of the city is **Mary Arden's Farm** ① *Wilmcote, Apr-Oct daily 1000-1700*, which was Shakespeare's mother's home. This property offers the experience of an authentic working Tudor farm, and 2013 is its 500th anniversary. Wilmcote railway station is just opposite the farm, or there is parking available.

In complete contrast, there's **Falstaff's Experience/Tudor World** ① *40 Sheep St, T01789-298070, www.falstaffexperience.co.uk, Mon-Sat 1030-1730, £6, children £3, concessions £4.50*, a gimmicky place that tries to bring Shakespeare's world to life by the power of animatronics and weird smells in one of the most historical properties in Stratford. It's probably a bit more immediate and tangible for kids than a five-hour session in the theatre watching the Dane play out his terrible fate, but one can't help feeling these operations somehow cheapen history. Ghost tours also available.

Next, pay a visit to the **MAD Museum** (Mechanical, Art and Design Museum) ① *Sheep St, T01789-269356, www.themadmuseum.co.uk, Oct-Mar daily 1100-1700, Apr-Sep daily 1030-1830, £6.80, children £4.50, concessions £5.50, family £19*, a small but fascinating museum displaying machines and mechanical paraphernalia, art, contraptions and gizmos.

Rejoining the Shakespeare Trail should now be your top priority. **Holy Trinity Church** ① *Old Town Stratford, T01789-266316, www.stratford-upon-avon.org, Mar and Oct Mon-Sat 0900-1700, Sun 1230-1700; Apr-Sep Mon-Sat 0830-1800, Sun 1230-1700; Oct-Feb Mon-Sat 0900-1600, Sun 1230-1700, Shakespeare's Grave £2, children £1, students 50p*, is well worth the entrance fee. Seeing Shakespeare's tomb and monument isn't the only reason for visiting. The church is right next to the River Avon, and its setting and distinguished architecture give it a justifiable claim to be one of England's loveliest parish churches.

Another great way to spend some time is by following the **River Avon Trail**, a great place to stroll or cycle through the town to the west, with great views of the theatre and thatched cottages.

The Vale of Evesham → *For listings, see pages 45-48.*

Easily reached from Birmingham on the A435 or from Oxford in the south on the A44, the area around Evesham produces most of the country's fruits. The optimum time for experiencing what has been dubbed the '**Blossom Trail**', is from late March to early May. The plum orchards explode with colour first, rapidly followed 10 to 14 days later by the apple blossoms. This is also the place to taste probably the best asparagus in the world, which is cheap, available in virtually every pub, restaurant and hotel in the area and served, in the local style, with brown bread and plenty of delicious butter.

Evesham

Evesham itself is a bustling market town with its roots going back to well before the Middle Ages. It owes its beginnings to a humble swineherd called Eoves who, in AD 709, had a vision of the Virgin Mary while searching for an escaped pig in an area called the 'Lomme'. Unable to believe his eyes, he persuaded his boss, Ecgwin, Bishop of Worcester, to come and have a look. The bishop was so impressed by the quality of the vision and the general holiness of the location that he decided to build a great Abbey there, which at the height of its power was one of the three most important religious sites in the country.

The River Avon has always played a central part in the history of the town and in the 19th century became the chief reason for the town becoming so popular with Victorian day trippers, who saw messing about on the water as a healthy, wholesome outdoor pursuit akin to cycling and walking. To this day there's a plethora of boating activities on offer: one of the best is a trip aboard the *Handsam Too* (T01386-834070), which can be boarded in Abbey Park, right next to the Almonry and **Tourist Information Centre** ① *Abbey Gate, T01386-446944, Mar-Oct Mon-Sat 1000-1700, Sun 1400-1700*. The **Almonry Heritage Centre** ① *www.almonryevesham.org, Mar-Oct Mon-Sat 1000-1700, Sun 1400-1700, £3, concessions £2, under-11s free*, is a wonderful and extremely well-preserved 14th-century building which used to be the home of the almoner of the eighth-century Benedictine Abbey. It now contains a museum spread out over a warren of 12 rooms which reflect the town's history, including the 13th-century Battle of Evesham, and excavated Anglo-Saxon treasure.

Evesham Abbey was largely dismantled at the orders of Henry VIII in 1540, but the twin churches of All Saints and St Lawrence and Abbot Lichfield's fine 16th-century bell tower still remain. These buildings within the Abbey precincts form an impressive backdrop to the **Abbey Park** with its grassy banks, shady trees and flower beds sweeping down to the river. The Battle of Evesham, the last skirmish of the Baron's War against an autocratic monarchy, was fought here in 1265. De Montfort led the charge for the Barons but was defeated by Edward, Henry III's son. His body was hacked to pieces and sent to the far-flung corners of the Kingdom. However, the monks of the Abbey were able to save a fragment of De Montfort's remains, which were buried with due ceremony before the High Altar of the Abbey, a spot now commemorated by a simple stone memorial.

North of the Cotswolds listings

For hotel and restaurant price codes and other relevant information, see pages 10-13.

● Where to stay

Stratford-upon-Avon *p41, map p42*

££££ The Arden Hotel, Waterside, T01789-298682, www.theardenhotelstratford.com. An elegant and sophisticated hotel following its multi-million pound refurbishment. Directly opposite the Royal Shakespeare Theatres.

££££ The Legacy Falcon, Chapel St, T00844-411 9005, www.legacy-hotels.co.uk. A very comfortable, pleasant and historical hotel with a cosy bar and lounge.

££££ Macdonald Alveston Manor, Clopton Bridge, on the way out of the town on the Oxford Rd, T0844-879 9138, www. macdonaldhotels.co.uk. One of the finest hotels in Stratford, it enjoys a spectacular view of the river, has its own grounds and is within walking distance of the theatre.

£££ Best Western Grosvenor Hotel, Warwick Rd, T0845-776 7676. A nice example of this hotel chain, located in a Grade II-listed building.

£££ Mercure Shakespeare Hotel, Chapel St, T01789-294997, www.mercure.com. Grade I-listed Tudor building in a central location. Has a good lounge area and a cosy atmosphere and promises luxurious accommodation a stone's throw from all the town's attractions.

£££ The Stratford, Arden St, T01789-271000, www.qhotels.co.uk. A handsome Victorian townhouse that has been refurbished into a superior boutique hotel.

£££ Stratford Manor, Warwick Rd, T01789-731173, www.qhotels.co.uk. A very tidy, modern building, set in 21 acres of grounds, with a spa.

£££ The White Swan, Rother St, T01789-297022, www.white-swan-stratford.co.uk. Stylish and historic, this recently renovated hotel has some truly stunning rooms.

£££-££ Caterham Guest House, 58/59 Rother St, T01789-267309, www. caterhamhousehotel.co.uk. Individual character rooms in the heart of Stratford.

££ Avonlea Guest House, 47 Shipston Rd, T01789-205940, www.avonlea-stratford. co.uk. Under new ownership since 2011, this B&B offers modern, stylish and comfortable guest rooms.

£ Forget-Me-Not Guest House, 18 Evesham Pl, T01789-204907, www. forgetmenotguesthouse.co.uk. With 5 en-suite rooms, this comfortable, cosy guesthouse is a bargain.

££ Greenhaven Guest House, 217 Evesham Rd, T01789-294874. Pleasant, modern rooms in a 4-star guesthouse.

£ Travelodge Stratford-upon-Avon, 251 Birmingham Rd, T0871-984 6414. A basic but very affordable hotel a mile away from the city centre.

Self-catering

41 & 42 Shakespeare St, T01789-298141. £650 per week high season, £250 in low season. Two 3-bed apartments within easy walking distance of the centre. With off-street parking.

Lysander Court, Ely St, T01789-730275. This central townhouse accommodates 2-4 people. Minimum 2-night stay.

Caravans and camping

Riverside Park, Tiddington Rd, T01789-292313, www.stratfordcaravans.co.uk. This accommodation park offers fantastic 'snugs' – the wooden equivalent to tents – situated in a meadow overlooking the river, as well as standard caravans and lodges. Open Mar-Nov.

Vale of Evesham *p44*

££££-£££ The Wood Norton, Worcester Rd, Evesham, T01386-765611, www.the woodnorton.com. Definitely the poshest hotel in the region, this place has 19th-century French-inspired interiors and simple, luxurious rooms. A beautiful grade II-listed Victorian building nestling in 170 acres of glorious parkland, it's undoubtedly the best place to experience the Vale in bloom. There is a restaurant here too that produces quality food from locally sourced ingredients.

££ The Stables, The Old Wheatsheaf Inn, High St, Old Badsey, Evesham, T01386-830380. Handily attached to a pub, this lovely old inn is a superior B&B with the advantage of a really classic drinking house next door.

££-£ Premier Inn Evesham, Evesham Country Park, off A46, Evesham, T0871-527 8384. Clean rooms and conveniently located, this recently refurbished hotel is a good example of the ubiquitous chain.

❼ Restaurants

Stratford-upon-Avon *p41, map p42*
Stratford restaurants are an amiable mix of beautiful country pubs – some of which have had the 'gastro' makeover – and smart, if a little old-school, silver service-type establishments. And, of course, this being the Midlands, there are plenty of curry houses to choose from.

££ Bamboodle, Union St, T01789-414999. Serving Asian-style street food in modern, upmarket surroundings; live music on Fri.

££ El Greco, Rother St, T01789-290505. Excellent Greek food in this contemporary restaurant overlooking the market square.

££ Essence, Old Red Lion Court, Bridge St, T01789-269999. Modern British, both in terms of the food and the decor. Good quality ingredients and an excellent wine list to accompany them.

££ Lamb's Restaurant, Sheep St, T01789-292554. Stylish and modern, this popular restaurant still retains a cosy feel in one of the oldest buildings in Stratford.

££ Marlowe's Restaurant, 1st floor, 18 High St, T01789-204999. A stunning, late 16th-century building with an Elizabethan dining room, though it is rather formal and prides itself on its silver service.

££ The Opposition Bistro, Sheep St, T01789-269980. Modern, bustling bistro in a historical building.

££ Sorrento, 8 Ely St, T01789-297999. Italian trattoria, simply but elegantly decorated with a pleasant easy-going atmosphere.

££ Thespians, 26 Sheep St, T01789-267187, www.thespiansltd.com. There's an army of smiling, extremely courteous staff in this place which, despite its name, specializes in north Indian and Bangladeshi cuisine.

£ Aladdin's, Tiddington Main St, Tiddington Rd, T01789-294491. Friendly curry house, reasonably priced, recommended by locals.

Cafés
Box Brownie Coffee, Henley St.
Nice little café that does great coffee.

❼ Pubs, bars and clubs

Stratford-upon-Avon *p41, map p42*
The College Arms, Lower Quinton, T01789-720342. An historic 16th-century inn on the edge of the Cotswolds, originally owned by Henry VIII.

Dirty Duck, Waterside, T01789-297312. The ultimate luvvies pub in Stratford, frequented by members of the RSC and the multitude of hangers-on that the theatre world has always attracted.

The Encore, Bridge St, T01789-269462. Stylish gastropub near the river.

Garrick Inn, High St, T01789-292186. This is the place to come if you like your pubs seriously beautiful and like a movie set from Olde Englande. The beer's not bad, either.

The Lamplighter, Rother St, T01789-293071. Traditional local pub, with beer garden, opposite the Civic Hall.

The Old Thatch Tavern, Greenhill St, T01789-295216. Small, homely little pub that has been a licensed premises since 1623. Nice little courtyard garden, very popular for food.

Othello's, Chapel St, T01789-269427. Upmarket bar and brasserie attached to the Mercure Shakespeare.

Pen and Parchment, Bridgefoot, T01789-297697. A traditional pub with a contemporary twist, and a large beer garden.
The Vintner, 4-5 Sheep St, T01789-297259. A wine bar – as you might expect – and restaurant, named for the vintner who lived in this building in 1600.
The Windmill Inn, Church St, T01789-297687. Friendly Greene King pub with a network of cosy, really picturesque rooms that are begging to be occupied for at least an entire day of supping cask ales.

⊕ Entertainment

Stratford-upon-Avon *p41, map p42*
Music
The Bandstand on the Recreation Ground has bands on some Sun afternoons during the summer.
Civic Hall, 14 Rother St, box office T01789-414513, www.civichall.co.uk. The venue for variety shows, classical music, big band, pantomime and dance nights. Licensed bar.

Theatre
Royal Shakespeare Company, www.rsc.org.uk, ticket hotline T0844-8001110, Mon-Sat 1000-1800, £14-60, discounts available.

⊛ Festivals

Stratford-upon-Avon *p41, map p42*
Apr Shakespeare's Birthday Celebrations. Morris dancing, street entertainers, the ceremony of the unfurling of the flags, the floral procession of dignitaries from all over the world between the Birthplace and Holy Trinity Church, dancing by local children and much more.
May Stratford-upon-Avon English Music Festival, held biennially, an extravaganza of all kinds of music.
Jun Stratford Regatta, on the River Avon.
Jul Stratford-upon-Avon International Flute Festival, free, lasts for about a fortnight.
Oct Stratford Mop Fair. The central streets of Stratford are closed to traffic for this annual traditional street fair with fairground rides, stalls, and the roasting of a whole ox, the first piece of which is auctioned for charity by the Mayor. It is one of the biggest mop fairs in the country.

⊙ Shopping

Stratford-upon-Avon *p41, map p42*
Antiques
The Barn Antiques Centre 5 miles from Stratford, T01789-721399. The largest antique centre in south Warwickshire, it's crammed full of collectables, bygones and antiques.

Clothes
Stratford-upon-Avon has a surprisingly decent collection of clothes shops. You'll find many of the usual high-street fashion staples on Bridge, Shrieve and Wood streets. If you're in need of 'fashion therapy', try **Gemini** at 15 Wood St, or **Gemini Shoes**, 3 Cook's Alley, where the proprietor offers healing hands for the fashion traumatized. **Littlejohn**, on Wood St, is a retailer that stocks only items designed in the UK, or supplied by UK companies. For something a bit different, try **Humbug Vintage** on Shreive Walk, which is home to hand-picked vintage items from around the world, but is still pretty affordable. For trinkets or foodie gifts, look for **Vinegar Hill** on Meer St; **Vin Neuf** on Union St; **Benson's House of Tea** on Henley St, or the **The Stratford Sweet Shop**, Henley St.

Markets
Selling of a more basic kind happens at the famous traditional Chartered Markets (all over town, but particularly on Market Sq), which still take place every week throughout the year. Stratford has been a market place for centuries, receiving its charters over 800 years ago. **The Farmer's Market** takes place twice monthly on Market Sq, just off Rother St, where you can buy superb fresh produce from some of the best farming land in the country.

🅞 What to do

Stratford-upon-Avon *p41, map p42*
Air
Wickers World Balloon Flights,
launch from the Stratford-upon-Avon
race course, Luddington Rd, T01889-
882222, www.wickersworld.co.uk.

Boating
Avon Boating, The Boathouse, Swan's
Nest Ln, T01789-267073. Hire small
boats or take a passenger cruise from
this 100-year old boathouse.
Bancroft Cruisers,, Bridgefoot, T01789-
269669, for guided sightseeing cruises.

Golf
Ingon Manor Golf & Country Club,
Ingon Ln, T01789-731857.
Stratford Golf Club, Tiddington Rd,
T01789-205749.
Stratford Oaks, Bearley Rd, Snitterfield,
T01789-731980.

Gliding
Bidford Gliding Centre, Honeybourne Rd,
Bidford-on-Avon, T01789-778807.
Stratford-upon-Avon Gliding Club,
Snitterfield Airfield, Snitterfield Rd,
Bearley, T01789-731095.

Horse racing
Stratford-upon-Avon Racecourse,
Luddington Rd, T01789-267949.

Horse riding
WJ Pettigrew, Ettington Park Stables,
T01789-450653.
The Sport Horse Training Centre,
The Wolds, The Green, Snitterfield,
T01789-730222.

Tennis
Stratford Lawn Tennis Club,
Swan's Nest Ln, T01789-295801.

🅞 Transport

Stratford-upon-Avon *p41, map p42*
Bicycle
Stratford Bike Hire, Stratford Greenway,
Seven Meadows Rd, T07711-776340,
closed in winter.

Bus
Long distance National Express,
T08717-818178, run 3 direct services
per day from **London Victoria** and
one from **Birmingham** (1 hr).

Car
Enterprise Rent-A-Car, Unit 8, Swan Trade
Centre, T01789-403920; **Hertz Rent-a-car,**
Station Rd, T01789-298827.

Taxi
Ranks are situated in Wood St, Rother St
and Bridge St, at Bridgefoot and at the
railway station. **Shakespeare Taxis,**
17 Greenhill St, T01789-266100;
24/7 Taxis, Shottery, T01789-415668.

Train
Stratford Station is off the Alcester Rd.
For timetable details check www.stratford
station.com. There are **Chiltern Railways**
services to **London** every 2 hrs, and **London
Midland** trains to **Birmingham** are hourly.

🅞 Directory

Stratford-upon-Avon *p41, map p42*
Hospitals Stratford Hospital, Arden St,
T01789-205831. Minor injuries unit daily
0900-1700. **Warwick Hospital,** Lakin Rd,
Warwick, T01926-495321. 24 hr A&E. **Arden
Medical Centre,** Albany Rd, T01789-414942.
Post office: Henley St, T01789-268869.
Library Public library on Henley St,
T0300-555 8171. See page 43 for
details of Shakespeare Centre Library.
Police Rother St, T01789-414111.

Contents

Footprint features

Gloucestershire

The lion's share of quintessential stone towns and villages that define the Cotswolds are to be found in Gloucestershire. Crowds of visitors flock to the honeypots in the northeast of the county, but the southern region also has its share of delights. Gloucester is the county town, with one of the most wonderfully well-preserved cathedrals in the country. Its very different neighbour is the elegant Regency spa town of Cheltenham. Both sit on the western edge of the Cotswolds overlooking the Severn Valley. In the south of the county, hearty Cirencester is the regional capital, an ancient Roman town surrounded by river valleys. To its west, workaday Stroud nestles amid glorious scenery peppered with neolithic remains.

The northern Cotswolds are so popular that the roads in summer often become choked with coaches and cars. The scenery is almost as stunning in winter though; if anything, the warm yellowy-grey limestone-built villages (which become more and more honey-coloured in the north) look even prettier in clear winter sunshine. The trio of Bourton-on-the-Water, Stow-on-the-Wold and Moreton-in-Marsh are the top destinations, but many of the smaller villages also receive many visitors each year. It's not hard to see why: the combination of rolling little hills, sparkling streams and tidy old villages is hard to resist. They're also sprinkled with a variety of rewarding and carefully maintained attractions, especially gardens and great houses. The Indian dream of Sezincote is one of the most extraordinary, although even more eccentric is the collection of antique crafts and handiwork on display at delightful Snowshill Manor. To the northeast is Chipping Campden, one of the most distinctive and fiercely protected of Cotswold towns. To the west, the countryside becomes impossibly picturesque, especially around the villages of Stanway and Broadway.

Arriving in the North Cotswolds

Getting there Moreton-in-Marsh is on the London Paddington–Worcester **train** line. From London the M40/A44 is the most direct driving route, although the A44 is notoriously slow. Even so, Moreton-in-Marsh can usually be reached in two hours. ▶ *For further details, see Transport, page 65.*

Information Bourton-on-the-Water TIC ⓘ *Victoria St, Bourton-on-the-Water, T01451-820211, Nov-Mar Mon-Fri 0930-1600, Sat 0930-1630, Apr-Oct Mon-Fri 0930-1700, Sat 0930-0730.* **Chipping Campden TIC** ⓘ *The Old Police Station, High St, Chipping Campden, T01386-841206, Apr-Oct daily 0930-1700, Nov-Mar Mon-Thu 0930-1300, Fri-Sun 0930-1600.* **Winchcombe TIC** ⓘ *Town Hall, High St, T01242-602925, Apr-Oct daily 1000-1700, Nov-Mar Sat, Sun 1000-1600.* See also www.cotswolds.com.

Bourton-on-the-Water

Bourton-on-the-Water is one of the most typical and also the most touristy of Cotswolds villages and worth a look for all that. It has been making the most of its charms since it made its name by reducing itself to a ninth of its size in 1937, using the same stone and water as the village, similar small-scale trees and shrubs, and a model of the model at the **Model Village** ⓘ *T01451-820467, www.theoldnewinn.co.uk, £3.60, under-13s £2.80, over 60s £3.20.* The model was renovated and updated in 2011. Other attractions include **The Cotswold Motoring Museum** ⓘ *The Old Mill, T01451-821255, daily 1000-1800, £4.50, under-16s £3.20,* home to a variety of vintage vehicles. Another favourite, with over 500 sq ft of displays, is the **Model Railway** ⓘ *Box Bush, High St, T01451-820686, www.bourtonmodelrailway.co.uk, Jun-Aug 1100-1700, Sep-Dec and Feb-May Sat and Sun 1100-1700, Jan limited opening; £2.75, under 16s and concessions £2.25.* Small birds, as well as larger ones, such as penguins, pelicans and flamingos, can be seen at **Birdland Park** ⓘ *Rissington Rd, T01451-820480, www.birdland.co.uk, Apr-Oct daily 1000-1800, Nov-Mar daily 1000-1600, £8.25, under 16s £5.25.* Great fun is the **Dragonfly Maze** ⓘ *Rissington Rd, T01451-822251, www.thedragonflymaze.com, £3, under 12s and concessions £2.50,* a yew-tree maze with clues engraved in flagstones to help you find the centre – and the golden dragonfly. A more unusual visitor attraction is the **Perfumery Exhibition** ⓘ *Victoria St,*

The Cotswolds on foot

Walking is one of the best ways to see the countryside, and there are many footpaths to choose from. The **Cotswold Way** (www.nationaltrail. co.uk/cotswold) is a 102-mile route from Chipping Campden to Bath via the outskirts of Cheltenham. The walk can be completed in a week or less depending on your fitness. There is plenty of accommodation along the way, but it gets booked up quickly, especially during the summer months so make sure you plan well ahead if you want to do this walk. Alternatives include the **Gloucestershire Way**, which covers 100 miles from Tewkesbury to Chepstow via Winchcombe and the Forest of Dean; the **Warden's Way** and **Windrush Way**,

circular routes that link Winchcombe and Bourton-on-the-Water (26 miles in all); the **North Cotswold Diamond**, a 60-mile circular route around Stow-on-the-Wold taking in Chipping Campden, Moreton-in-Marsh and Northleach; the **Cheltenham Circular Footpath**, which circles the town of Cheltenham, and the **Wysis Way**, a 55-mile route linking the rivers Wye, Severn and Thames that runs from Monmouth via Gloucester to the source of the Thames near Kemble. **Cotswold Walks** ① *T01242-518888, www. cotswoldwalks.com*, is a local company specializing in self-guided and guided walks. **Compass Holidays** ① *T01242-250642*, organize luggage transfers and accommodation along the Cotswold Way.

T01451-820698, www.cotswold-perfumery.co.uk, daily 1000-1700, £5, concessions £3.50, which manufactures scents on site and also offers make-your-own perfume courses. Not accessible for wheelchair users.

Stow-on-the-Wold and around

A few miles up the A429, **Stow-on-the-Wold** is the capital of the Cotswolds, where most roads meet before heading off across the hills. (En route from Bourton, stop off at the **Slaughters**, Upper and Lower, a pair of impossibly twee little stone villages, just off the A429.) Stow's marketplace and side streets are busy in summer with crowds browsing the antique shops. Even so, along with **Moreton-in-Marsh**, 5 miles north, Stow has a more businesslike and workaday air than many Cotswold settlements, and both towns are surrounded by some of the region's most enticing destinations for a day out. Moreton's famous **Tuesday market** is still a sight to behold and the town benefits from being on the main London–Worcester railway.

Six miles east of Moreton, near the utterly idyllic village of Great Tew, the **Rollright Stones** are an eerie collection of standing stones. The King's Men and the Whispering Knights, as the two main groups are known, are shrouded in legends of their supernatural powers. They sit in a shrubby enclosure some distance from the solitary King Stone. This is apparently a petrified invading monarch who had been told by a wise old woman that he would rule the land if he could take seven strides and see Long Compton. Foiled by the lie of the land, he was turned to stone, some distance from his men and the knights plotting his downfall whatever the outcome.

Just west of Moreton, **Batsford Arboretum** ① *T01386-701441, daily 1000-1645, £7, under-16s £3*, is a 50-acre plot covered with rare and exotic shrubs and trees. Next door you'll find the **Cotswold Falconry Centre** ① *T01386-701043, www.cotswold-falconry.co.uk, Feb-Nov, £8, children £4, concessions £6*. Close by, beneath Bourton-on-the-Hill, **Sezincote**

① *T01386-700444, www.sezincote.co.uk, house May-Sep Thu, Fri and bank hols 1430-1730, £10, no children, gardens Jan-Nov Thu, Fri and bank hols 1400-1800, £5, children £1.50, no dogs,* is an even rarer wonder. This Indian-style house was the inspiration for the Brighton Pavilion. The extraordinary onion-domed affair was designed by SP Cockerell and is surrounded by an Oriental water garden.

Snowshill and Stanway

Stranger still is the collection of things gathered together at **Snowshill Manor** ① *(NT) T01386-842814, Mar-Jun, Aug-Nov Wed-Sun 1200-1700 (garden 1130-1730), Jul Mon 1130-1630, Wed-Sun 1200-1700, £9.40, under-16s £5.20, garden only £5, under 16s £2.60.* From the early 1920s the eccentric architect and craftsman Charles Wade amassed an array of ordinary domestic antiques, musical instruments, suits of armour, Japanese masks, tapestries, reliquaries and furniture among other things, the emphasis being on anything and everything individually hand-crafted. He himself lived in spartan conditions in the cottage next door as his insatiable antique-hunting crowded out the manor house itself. He also created a beautiful terraced and very intimate garden, which winds and descends from one 'room' to another, partial enclosures revealing his mysterious handmade miniatures. Wade gave the property to the National Trust on his death in 1956. Both house and gardens are surprising. Wade's equally astonishing costume collection, with which he used to surprise guests like Graham Greene, Virginia Woolf, JB Priestley and John Betjeman, can be seen by appointment at Berrington Hall, near Leominster in Herefordshire; phone ahead for details, T01568-613720.

A couple of miles away from Snowshill as the crow flies, **Stanton** and **Stanway** are a pair of delightful honey-coloured villages. Lord Neidpath has lovingly and imaginatively restored the garden at **Stanway House** ① *near Winchcombe, T01386-584469, Jun-Aug Tue, Thu 1400-1700, £7, under-14s £2.* The pyramid folly overlooks a 185-yard long waterfall as it cascades gently down from the canal, surrounded by fountains and dreamy gardens to wander through. Lord Neidpath is most accommodating if you wish to arrange a visit out of season. Close by, **Hailes Abbey** ① *(NT/EH), T01242-602398, Apr-Sep daily 1000-1700, Oct daily 1000-1600, £4.30, under-16s £2.60, concessions £3.90,* was a Cistercian monastery founded in 1246 by King Henry III's brother Richard, Earl of Cornwall, who was buried here in 1272; the monastery was dissolved in 1539. A series of leaping arches from its cloister are all that survive in a quiet Cotswold valley, complemented by a small museum documenting its history.

Broadway and Chipping Campden

Broadway is yet another contender for most beautiful village in the Cotswolds. A few miles north, Chipping Campden is not as commercialized as many parts of the Cotswolds and remains fiercely protective of the architectural legacy of the woollen boom and its sedate atmosphere. The gently curving and really quite grand High Street is a delight, surrounded by various styles of well-preserved terraced housing. The magnificent 15th-century church, built with the profits of the lucrative wool industry, has a stirring sky-bound tower, while the Market Hall, built in 1627, is the centrepiece of the town. Chipping Campden was also famous for the artisan centre set up in 1902 by Arts and Crafts designer CR Ashbee with workers relocated from the East End. The experiment failed in 1908 because, in those days, the town was too remote for the results of their labour to be effectively distributed. Chipping Campden is also the start of the 102-mile long-distance footpath to Bath – the **Cotswold Way** (see box, opposite).

Two miles north of Chipping Campden, **Hidcote Manor Garden** ① *(NT) T01386-438333, www.nationaltrust.org.uk/hidcote, check the website for opening times, £9.50, children £4.75,* is one of Britain's most extraordinary gardens. A maze of imaginative settings featuring high hedges and garden rooms of spectacular colour have been nurtured by Major Lawrence Johnson on what seemed to be hostile terrain in a windy and cold setting. It's a must-see, but often very busy in summer. Less busy but in many ways as rewarding is **Kiftsgate Court** ① *T01386-438777, May-Jul: Sat-Wed 1200-1800, Aug Sat-Wed 1400-1800, Sep and Apr Mon, Wed and Sun 1400-1800, £7.50, under-16s £2.50,* on the edge of Glyde Hill nearby. It's a superb hill garden, famous for the largest rosebush in Britain twisting up a copper beech tree.

Winchcombe and around

Heading southwest again on the beautiful B4632 towards Cheltenham from Broadway, Winchcombe was the ancient capital of the Anglo-Saxon kingdom of Mercia, with very old squat stone buildings and a prosperous air. Close by is 15th-century **Sudeley Castle** ① *T01242-604244, Mar-Nov daily 1030-1700, £12, under-16s £6.50, concessions £11, family £35,* which is a hot tourist destination and deserves its accolades. It boasts fantastic shrub roses in the Queen's garden, sculptured yews and pools in the grounds. The venerable and rambling home of the Dent-Brocklehursts has a long history; inside are slightly less absorbing displays of Victoriana and old master paintings. Close to Charlton Abbots, **Belas Knap** is the county's most impressive neolithic longbarrow, a superbly positioned chambered tomb for at least 30 people which has been opened up so that visitors can see inside. The B4632 continues southwest over beautiful **Cleeve Hill**, with its fabulous viewpoints, and past the racecourse of the Regency spa town of Cheltenham (see below), a very different kettle of fish from crumbly old Winchcombe.

Cheltenham and Gloucester → *For listings, see pages 62-66.*

These two very different towns of similar size lie within 6 miles of each other either side of the M5 Bristol–Birmingham motorway. To the east, Cheltenham is a very polite and conservative Regency spa town set in a bowl of the western Cotswolds. Famous for its hunting and horse-racing events, which draw huge horsey crowds, it also bills itself as a year-round festival town, building on the strengths of its world-famous music and literature events. It also has a surprisingly young population, thanks to the variety of colleges and schools based here. Gloucester could hardly be more different: an ancient county town, its magnificently preserved cathedral is the main draw, visible from afar, as well as its tiny Beatrix Potter museum. Its Victorian docks have been effectively redeveloped into a visitor attraction, featuring the Waterways Museum and an absorbing military museum. Otherwise Gloucester is not a particularly pretty sight, but the whole workaday city provides a refreshing counterbalance to Cheltenham.

Arriving in Cheltenham and Gloucester

Getting there There are frequent **trains** from London Paddington (two hours) to both towns. **First Great Western** have some direct services, otherwise change at Swindon; other operators include **Virgin** and **Central Trains**. There are also direct rail services to Gloucester from Bristol and the Southwest, Wales and the Midlands. **National Rail Enquiries** ① *T08457-484950*.

By road, from London take the M4 for approx 110 miles, then join the northbound M5 until junction 12 followed by the A38 which enters Gloucester from the south, alternatively you can exit the M5 at junction 11a to the west of the city. Approximate driving time: two hours 20 minutes; distance: 140 miles. The M40/A40 is the main route to Cheltenham, about two hours from London. By bus from Victoria coach station the journey is between three hours and four hours. Buses generally leave hourly throughout the day. **Traveline**, ① *www.travelinesw.com*. ➨ *For further details, see Transport, page 65.*

Getting around Cheltenham and Gloucester are small enough to **walk** around. In Cheltenham especially it's easily the best way to enjoy the town. **Buses** to the Cotswolds and outlying villages are run by **Stagecoach** ① *T01452-527516, www.stagecoachbus.com*. There are six bus routes from Gloucester to Cheltenham. For a fast journey, try the 94X along the Golden Valley bypass. Dayrider tickets are available from the driver offering a day's travel by **Stagecoach** buses.

Information Cheltenham TIC ① *77 Promenade, T01242-522878, www.visitcheltenham. com. Mon-Sat, 0930-1715 (Weds opens at 1000), bank holiday Mon 1000-1330*. Produces a good mini-guide to the town and is generally very helpful. Note that this centre will be relocating to the new Cheltenham Art Gallery and Museum development in mid-2013. **Gloucester TIC** ① *28 Southgate St, T01452-396572, www.gloucester.gov.uk/tourism. Tue-Sat 0930-1700, ad hoc Sundays*. Free accommodation booking service.

Cheltenham

The elegant Tunbridge Wells of the west, Cheltenham is a really very pretty town and it knows it. The medicinal properties of its waters were 'discovered' in the early 18th century, encouraging George III to spend more than a month in town sampling them for his health. Competing spas were developed in the early 19th century at Pittville (where the Pump

Room remains, still dispensing waters to the brave) and Montpellier, which is now the town's exclusive shopping strip. Cheltenham Ladies College was founded in 1841 for the education of young society girls and became one of the most exclusive girls' schools in the country. Cheltenham – with its stucco and limestone, shady tree-filled squares and crescents, delicate ironwork verandas and balconies – still presents, on a small scale, one of the most complete Regency townscapes in Britain, on a par with Bath and Edinburgh.

The wide and partly pedestrianized **Promenade** is the main drag, and the **Long Garden** to its west offers relaxation and a farmers' market every second and last Friday of the month. The TIC and bus station are tucked behind in front of **Royal Crescent**, a fine little

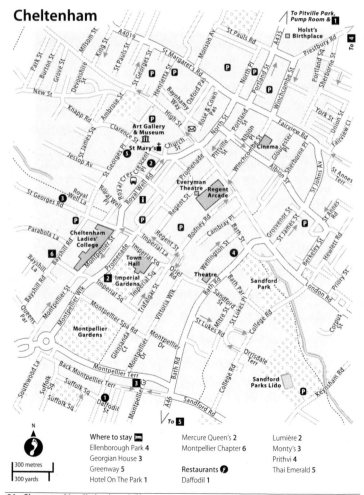

Cheltenham

Where to stay 🛏
Ellenborough Park **4**
Georgian House **3**
Greenway **5**
Hotel On The Park **1**

Mercure Queen's **2**
Montpellier Chapter **6**

Restaurants 🍴
Daffodil **1**

Lumière **2**
Monty's **3**
Prithvi **4**
Thai Emerald **5**

half-moon terrace built in 1805. A few steps north, on Clarence St, the **Cheltenham Art Gallery and Museum** ① *T01242-237431, www.cheltenhammuseum.org.uk.* is currently being redeveloped and is due to reopen in mid-2013. Check the website for details. Next to the museum's late-Victorian building stands Cheltenham's oldest survivor, the **church of St Mary's** with its severe stone spire. Five minutes' walk north up North St, the **birthplace** of the composer **Gustav Holst** ① *4 Clarence Rd, Pittville, T01242-524846, www.holstmuseum. org.uk, Feb-Jun and Oct-Dec Tue-Sat 1000-1600, Jul-Sep Tue-Sat 1000-1700, Sun 1330-1700, £4.50, concessions £4*, preserves his memory and his piano, as well as giving a glimpse inside a Regency terraced townhouse, with its cosy drawing room, nursery and working kitchen.

Continuing north along West Drive, past two dignified Georgian squares, Clarence and Wellington, a 20-minute walk brings you to **Pittville Park**, natural on the western side and more formal on the eastern side, divided by Evesham Road. The **Pump Room** ① *T01242-523852, Wed-Sun 1000-1600*, has been refurbished on the ground floor to show what it may have looked like when built in the 1820s as the centrepiece of Joseph Pitt's ambitious and ultimately failed development of Cheltenham's spa capacity. The waters can still be tasted here.

Heading south on the Promenade leads into the boutique shopping area of **Montpellier**, full of rare books and antiques, designer dress shops and jewellers. Beyond Imperial Square and the grand Edwardian Town Hall, where spa water is still dispensed in the foyer from a Royal Doulton urn, the Queen's Hotel's impressive colonnaded portico stands at the end of the Promenade, between the Imperial and Montpellier gardens. The famous 30 armless **Cheltenham ladies** then process down Montpellier Walk, a striking series of caryatids imitating the Acropolis and supporting the roof of Montpellier Arcade, an early shopping mall. At the end of the street, the Rotunda, now a bank, was the second of Cheltenham's spa developments.

Cheltenham Racecourse ① *www.cheltenham.co.uk*, is located just a short way to the north of the town and enjoys views of the rolling Cotswold Hills. Popular for its numerous race days and special events, the racecourse can be reached easily by car, coach, bus – and even by helicopter!

Gloucester

Cheltenham's workaday brother, the capital of Gloucestershire, may not be much to look at, either at its centre or on its outskirts, but the distant views of the **cathedral** ① *T01452-528095, www.gloucestercathedral.org.uk* (which featured in the Harry Potter film *The Philosopher's Stone*), are compensation enough. Close up, beneath its glorious Painswick-stone tower, the church turns out to be very well preserved. Standing proud on College Green, this is English Perpendicular architecture at its very best. Built over the course of a century with funds raised from pilgrims to the shrine of Edward II, the astonishing embellishment of the original Norman church began in the 1330s. Highlights of the interior are the huge Norman columns of the nave and the way that the 14th-century vaulting leaps around them, as well as the East window of the same date, the largest in Britain. Beyond the south transept the wooden effigy of William the Conqueror's eldest son, Robert, dates from around 1260. Robert died in 1134 imprisoned in Cardiff Castle by his younger brother, King Henry I. On the other side of the fabulous vaulted choir is the tomb of Edward II, horribly murdered in Berkeley Castle in 1327. The exquisite Lady Chapel is the most recent major structural alteration to the fabric of the cathedral, built in the late 15th-century and artfully designed not to obscure the East window. The cathedral's other unmissable sight is the late 14th-century cloisters with their extraordinary fan vaulted tracery.

Close by, **The House of the Tailor of Gloucester** ① *9 College Ct, T01452-422856, www. tailor-of-gloucester.org.uk, Mon-Sat 1000-1700, Sun 1200-1600*, is popular with Beatrix Potter fans: a tiny little museum and shop in the original house sketched by the author for her favourite story. A short 10-minute walk west down College St past Robert Smirke's Shire Hall of 1816 brings you to England's deepest inland port and terminus of the canal to Sharpness: the **Gloucester Docks**. Here, in a converted Victorian warehouse, is the **Waterways Museum** ① *T01452-318200, daily 1100-1600, £4.95/£10 with boat, children £3.50/£7 with boat, concessions £3.95/£8 with boat*, which should satisfy the most curious of canal fans with its array of interactive displays and working models illustrating the history of the first industrial revolution's transport network. The museum also runs regular boat trips on the **Gloucester and Sharpness Canal**. At the other end of the docks, the **Soldiers of Gloucestershire Museum** ① *daily 1000-1700, closed Mon Oct-mid Mar, £4.75, under-16s £2.75, concessions £3.25*, tells the absorbing story of the lives (and deaths) of Gloucestershire soldiers over the last 300 years. Over the water, on the other side of the main basin, the **Antiques Centre** ① *T01452-529716, Mon-Sat 1000-1700, Sun 1100-1700*, provides room for a host of different stallholders in another converted warehouse, with 70 different shops.

Back in the centre of town, the **Gloucester City Museum and Art Gallery** ① *Brunswick Rd, T01452-396131*, and the **Folk Museum** ① *Westgate St, T01452-396868, Tue-Sat 1000-1700, £3, £2 concessions*, are worth a visit. The huge Victorian city museum houses a lively and well-presented collection of dinosaur models, archaeology, furniture and Gloucestershire arts and crafts; the chocolate-box façade of the Folk Museum is home to one of the oldest-established collections dedicated to social history. A couple of miles north of the city centre, at **Wallsworth Hall** ① *Twigworth, T01452-731422, www.nature-in-art.org.uk, Tue-Sun 1000-1700, £5.25, concessions £4.75*, is a Georgian mansion dedicated to the Nature in Art exhibition, with some interesting displays.

South Cotswolds → *For listings, see pages 62-66.*

Much less tourist-tramped and slightly less picturesque than the northern Cotswolds, the area south of the A40 between Northleach and Cirencester is prosperous commuter country. Northleach once rivalled Chipping Campden in wool wealth and remains fairly unspoiled. Cirencester was a very important Roman town and is still a confident regional centre blessed with another beautiful church, marketplace and a clutch of 17th- and 18th-century houses. To its west, Stroud was once a thriving centre for the first industrial revolution. A few impressive cloth mills still stand, but its major draw is the spectacular rolling scenery all around which affords wonderful views at every turn.

Arriving in the South Cotswolds

Getting there Kemble and Stroud are on the main London to Bristol and South Wales lines via Gloucester; change at Swindon. Regular trains take just over two hours. By road from London the M4/A419 via Swindon is the quickest route to Cirencester taking about two hours. An alternative would be the M40/A40/A429, sometimes much less congested.

Information Cirencester TIC ① *Corinium Museum, Park St, T01285-654180, Apr-Oct Mon-Sat 1000-1700, Sun 1400-100, Nov-Mar Mon-Sat 1000-1600, Sun 1400-1600.* **Malmesbury TIC** ① *The Town Hall, Cross Hayes, T01666-823748, Oct-Mar Mon-Thu 0900-1650, Fri 0900-1620, Apr-Sep also Sat 1000-1600.* **Stroud TIC** ① *George St, T01453-760960.*

Northleach

West of Burford in Oxfordshire (see page 32), the A40 heads into Gloucestershire up the Windrush valley. After 9 miles it bypasses **Northleach**, in the Middle Ages the most prosperous of the Cotswold wool towns. Today, it's much less commercialized than many, and its magnificent church survives as a reminder of its glory days. The **church of St Peter and St Paul** is more impressive on the outside than in, with its great porch, tower and battlements, but the brasses paid for by rich wool merchants are exceptional. The town's other unmissable attraction is the **World of Mechanical Music** ① *The Oak House, High St, T01451-860181, www.mechanicalmusic.co.uk, daily 1000-1700, £8, concessions £7, children £3.50,* a hymn to self-playing musical instruments, from tiny singing birds in snuff boxes to grand pianolas, rare clocks, musical boxes, automata and mechanical music machines; visitors are often lucky enough to be shown round by the collection's enthusiastic owner, Keith Harding.

Three miles south of Northleach, in a wooded valley near Yanworth is the **Chedworth Roman Villa** ① *(NT), T01242-890256, Feb-Mar and Oct-Nov daily 1000-1600, Apr-Sep 1000-1700, £8.80, children £4.40, family £22.00.* The surprisingly extensive remains of a rich Roman's house, the site includes floor mosaics (some of which have only been excavated very recently), two bathhouses and a hypocaust. There's also a newly refurbished museum of finds from the site, which as a whole is a kind of museum of Victorian archaeology in itself.

Bibury and Barnsley

Bibury, about 5 miles southeast of Chedworth, is another of the Cotswolds' picture-postcard villages, a peaceful string of stone-built cottages nestling beside the little river Coln. Arlington Row, a terrace of cottages purpose-built for weavers in the 17th century, must be some of the most photographed in the county. There's also a mill museum, several teashops and some good pubs.

Heading towards Cirencester from Bibury, the pretty B4425 fetches up after 3 miles in Barnsley. There's less to see here, as far as the village is concerned (although the pub has a formidable reputation for its food), instead the big draw is **Barnsley House** ① *T01285-470000*, with its wonderful garden created by pioneering TV gardener Rosemary Verey. Now an exclusive boutique hotel (see Where to stay, page 63), the gardens are open to guests of the hotel restaurant and of the pub in the village (for both; see below).

Cirencester and around

Cirencester is the most important town in the southern Cotswolds, an ancient meeting of the roads and still a thriving, good-looking market town with a hearty complement of agriculture students. The Roman town of 'Corinium' was second only to Colchester and London in importance; retired legionaries were settled here, and the grassy remains of their amphitheatre can still be seen west of the town. The **Corinium Museum** ① *Park St, T01285-655611, www. coriniummuseum.cotswold.gov.uk, Mon-Sat 1000-1700, Sun 1400-1700, £4.95, children £2.45, concessions available*, offers a quite exceptional insight into their way of life, easily comprehensible to kids, as well as displaying the famous Hunting Dogs and Four Seasons mosaics, along with other finds from the area. Otherwise, 'Siren,' as the locals call it, is good place for browsing around in the old marketplace. Its mini-cathedral of a church testifies to the wealth it once enjoyed from wool in the 15th century.

Northwest of Cirencester, the delightful valley of the Dunt is lined with adorable villages called 'Duntisbourne-something'. At **Duntisbourne Rouse** the tiny Norman church is in a charming situation and has a remarkable ancient lychgate. Excellent walks lead through rolling, well-hedged countryside towards **Sapperton**, where the tunnel for the canal is the one of the longest in the country. The tunnel runs beneath the Cotswolds for almost 3 miles, emerging close to the **source of the River Thames** near Kemble. There's not much to see except for a headstone at this mystical spot in a lonely field – Old Father Thames keeps shifting his ground. Close by at **Rodmarton Manor** ① *T01285-841442 May-Sep Wed, Sat & bank hols 1400-1700, £8, children £4*, there's a stunning garden designed by Ernest Barnsley and Claud Biddulph in the 19th century. The Arts and Crafts design has topiary punctuating the natural circumference of the garden rooms. Roses bushes and herbaceous borders lead towards the woodland walks.

Further down the A433 is **Tetbury**, a well-heeled small town with royal connections: Prince Charles' Highgrove Estate is just down the road. Five miles southwest of Tetbury on the A433 is **Westonbirt Arboretum** ① *T01666-880220, www.forestry.gov.uk/westonbirt, Mon-Fri 0900-1800, Sat and Sun 0800-1800 (Apr-Aug until 2000), check website for admission prices*, which covers 600 acres of landscaped grounds. Some 17 miles of paths run through a collection of over 18,000 trees begun in 1829 by Robert Holford, who made his fortune piping clean drinking water into London. Westonbirt is magnificent at any time of year but is at its dizzying best in autumn, when the leafy, sunlit glades become a thousand luminous hues, from lustrous gold to flaming scarlet and blazing orange. Weekends can get very busy, so come during the week for a more peaceful visit.

Stroud

Sapperton's canal heads on west towards Stroud, once an important woollen mill town, now something a hotbed of 'green' thinking. Not much to look at itself, the town is surrounded by spectacular scenery: villages clinging to escarpments, wooded hills and rolling fields. The **Elliott Nature Reserve** on Swift's Hill, just outside Slad, affords some of the finest views in Gloucestershire. More spectacular views can be had from the roofed longbarrow called **Hetty Pegler's Tump** (or Uley Long Barrow) in winter, while **Ulebury Iron Age Hill Fort** on the Cotswold Way also presents far-reaching vistas towards Wales. Near the **Nimpsfield** an unroofed longbarrow looks over the Severn Estuary into Wales, as does the Coaley Peak Picnic Site, part of a swathe of land at over 400 ft.

    Painswick Rococo Garden ⓘ *T01452-813204, www.rococogarden.org.uk, Jan-Oct 1100-1700, £6.50, children £3, concessions £5.50*, is a delightful journey into the past following the uncovering and restoration of a garden from a 1748 painting by Thomas Robins. Gothic houses with sculptures, frescos and alcoves and pools are dotted throughout, joined by winding paths. The informal rococo style is brilliantly eye-catching and imaginative.

Gloucestershire listings

For hotel and restaurant price codes and other relevant information, see pages 10-13.

● Where to stay

North Cotswolds *p51*

££££ Buckland Manor Hotel, Buckland, nr Broadway, T01386-852626, www.buckland manor.co.uk. A 13th-century manor house surrounded by a 10-acre garden with 13 bedrooms, a putting green, swimming pool, tennis and croquet lawns.

££££ Cotswold House Hotel, Chipping Campden, T01386-840330, www.cotswold house.com. This Edwardian manor house has luxurious contemporary rooms, a townhouse garden and a spa.

££££ Dormy House, Willersey Hill, Broadway, nr Cheltenham, T01386-852711, www.dormyhouse.co.uk. This 17th-century farmhouse is set high on Willersey Hill looking over the Cotswolds. Rooms are welcoming, with fresh flowers and oversized club chairs. Its 2 restaurants use high-quality local ingredients.

££££ Lords of the Manor Hotel, Upper Slaughter, nr Cheltenham and Stow-on-the-Wold, T01451-820243, www.lordsof themanor.com. This former rectory built in 1650 and is set in one of the prettiest villages in the Cotswolds. It's home to a Michelin-starred restaurant and has meticulously manicured gardens, riding, tennis and croquet on offer.

££££ Lower Slaughter Manor, Lower Slaughter, T01451-820456, www.lower slaughter.co.uk. This manor house was built in 1651 on the site of a 1068 Domesday manor. It has a lavish, award-winning fine-dining restaurant and 19 well-appointed rooms.

££££ The Noel Arms Hotel, High St, Chipping Campden, T01386-840317, www.noelarmshotel.com. 28 unique rooms, dog-friendly, with a coffee shop, bar and restaurant. The restaurant hosts an award-winning curry night once a month.

££££-£££ Wyck Hill House Hotel & Spa Wyck Hill, near Stow-on-the-Wold, T01451-830141. Former 19th-century lodge transformed into a tranquil home with flowers from the garden dotted throughout.

£££ The Crown Inn & Hotel, High St, Blockley, Moreton-in-Marsh, T01386-700245, www.crownhotelblockley.co.uk. A family-run coaching inn. Put your feet up in front of a roaring fire and enjoy a pint before a meal in the rated 'Rafters' restaurant

£££ King's Head Inn, The Green, Bledington, nr Stow-on-the-Wold, T01608-658365, www.thekingsheadinn.net. A 16th-century inn, which used to be a cider house, in an idyllic setting. Burbling brooks and quacking ducks surround this stone inn with its exposed beams, benches and fireplaces. The comfortable bedrooms are located in the annexe off the courtyard.

£££ The Malt House, Broad Campden, nr Chipping Campden, T01386-840295, www.malt-house.co.uk. This welcoming and comfortable former 18th-century malt house is now a family-run guesthouse with an eye for detail. Roaring fires. The hosts oversee breakfast made from their own garden fruits.

££ Guiting Guest House, Post Office La, Guiting Power, T01451-850470, www. guitingguesthouse.com. This former farmhouse has been tastefully transformed into a guesthouse using local stone and timber. Open fires make it cosy and informal.

££ The Royalist Hotel, Digbeth St, Stow-on-the-Wold, T01451-830670, www.theroyalisthotel.com. Supposedly the oldest inn in the country. Owned by the Knights of St John in AD 947 and then used as an almshouse. Beams, fireplaces, nooks and crannies abound.

££ Westward, Westward Sudeley Lodge, Winchcombe, T01242-604372, www. westward-sudley.co.uk. Looking over Sudeley Castle, this Georgian manor house has grand formal gardens and perfect lawns. 3 guest rooms are available in this family home.

£ Rectory Farm, Rectory Farm, Salford, near Chipping Norton, T01608-643209, www.rectoryfarm.info. This 18th-century farmhouse is set in an uninhabited 450-acre valley. There are well-stocked trout-fishing lakes on the property.

£ YHA, Stow-on-the-Wold, T0845-3719540.

Cheltenham *p55, map p56*
££££ Ellenborough Park, Southam Rd, T01242-807520, www.ellenborough park.com. Old house situated in the original racecourse estate, 10 mins from the town centre. This exemplary hotel has lavish rooms.

££££ The Greenway, Shurdington, T01242-862352, www.thegreenway hotelandspa.com. Built in 1584, this 21-bedroom Elizabethan manor house has formal grounds and a croquet pitch. The coach house is more modern but perhaps more spacious and quieter.

££££ Hotel On The Park, Evesham Rd, T01242-518898, www.thehoteluk.co.uk. A stylish Regency townhouse, 6 mins' walk from the centre of Cheltenham. The rooms are beautifully decorated with fine linens and antiques.

££££-£££ The Montpellier Chapter, Bayshill Rd, T01242-527788, www.the montpellierchapterhotel.com. 5 mins' walk from the town centre, a Regency townhouse with a cheerful atmosphere and clean, comfortable rooms.

£££ Georgian House, 77 Montpellier Terr, T01242-515577, www.georgianhouse. net. Across the park from fashionable Montpellier, this house lives up to its name and has individually designed bedrooms.

£££ Mercure Queen's Hotel, The Promenade, T08700-4008107, www.mercure.com. A 4-star historic hotel done up in faintly characterless style but in a superb position bang in the middle of things.

££ Strozzi Palace Boutique Suites, 55 St Georges Pl, T01242-650028, www.strozzipalace.co.uk. Stylish, Italian-inspired suites at a great-value price.

South Cotswolds *p59*
££££ Barnsley House Barnsley, nr Cirencester, T01285-470000, www.barnsley house.com. This stunning boutique hotel is housed in a beautiful Cotswold building, surrounded by beautiful, intimate gardens, complete with luxurious spa. Rooms combine traditional elements with ultra-contemporary facilities and styling. The Potager Restaurant is open to non-guests.

££££ Calcot Manor, nr Tetbury, T01666-890391, www.calcotmanor.co.uk. Dating back to the 14th century, this manor house with extensions is in the heart of the Cotswolds. There's a converted 16th-century barn and courtyard, and a top restaurant.

££££-£££ Bibury Court Hotel, Bibury, T01285-740337, www.biburycourt.com. A lovely Jacobean mansion with a venerable history. The river runs through its fine back garden (a good place to take afternoon teas) and there's a gate into the churchyard from the orchards. Enjoy river walks into Bibury and up to Coln St Aldwyns. The rooms are comfortable and the restaurant has a good reputation.

££££-£££ The New Inn at Coln, Coln-St-Aldwyns, T0844-8153434, www.new-inn. co.uk. This old coaching inn dates back to the 16th century. The inn has an award-winning restaurant with a garden that's lovely in summer.

£££ The Cotswolds88 Hotel, Kemps La, Painswick, T01452-813688, www. cotswolds88hotel.com. Luxury rooms with great views of the Cotswold Hills. Masterclasses in cookery are available at the cooking school.

£££ Hatton Court, Upton Hill, Upton St, Leonard's, nr Painswick, T01452-617412, www.hatton-court.co.uk. Overlooking the Severn Valley, this 17th-century manor house has peerless views. Have drinks or tea on the terrace overlooking the woodlands below.

£££ Swan Hotel at Bibury, Bibury, T01285-740695, www.cotswolds-inns-hotels.co.uk. Built in the 17th century, this hotel overlooks the river. Expect terry white robes and cotton bath sheets. Restaurant with awards and a good wine list.

£££ The Village Pub, Barnsley, nr Cirencester, T01285-740421, www.thevillagepub.co.uk. Comfortable contemporary rooms are offered in a handsome refurbished boozer that's not much like your average local. There's top-quality food on the menu and complimentary access to Barnsley House gardens (across the road) for guests (see above).

£££ Winstone Glebe, Winstone, near Cirencester, T01285-821451, www.winstoneglebe.com. This B&B is a former Georgian rectory set in 5 acres of garden and fertile grazing land. The proprietor is also a professional chef.

££ 1 Cove House, Ashton Keynes, south of Cirencester, T01285-861226, www.covehouse.co.uk. Expect a hearty greeting at this 16th-century manor house which has 2 beautiful en suite bedrooms and lovely gardens.

££ The Falcoln Hotel, Painswick, T01452-814222, www.falcolnpainswick.co.uk. Small but comfortable and welcoming hotel with church views and a restaurant.

££ The Rose and Crown, Nympsfield, Stonehouse, T01453-860240, www.therose andcrowninn.com. Clean, comfortable rooms in this refurbished pub near Uley.

Owlpen Manor, Owlpen, near Uley, T01453-860816, www.owlpen.com. 9 self-catering cottages (sleeping 2-9, from £280 per week up to £20 per person per week). This splendid building dates from the 13th-century. With its long and romantic history, it is gutsy and rarefied. As to be expected, the cottages are appointed with the fabrics and furniture of an English country house and are well-stocked with amenities.

Restaurants

North Cotswolds *p51*
See also Where to stay, above.

£££ Lygon Arms Hotel, High St, Broadway, T01386-852255. Choose between the *Goblet's Bistro* for brasserie style lunches and the splendid oak-panelled *Great Hall* restaurant for dinner at this renowned member of the Puma Hotel group.

££ Baker's Arms, Broad Campden, T01386-840515. Good value bar food in a pretty village pub.

££ The Craven Arms, Brockhampton, T01242-820410. Real ale destination pub with a large garden, good bar snacks and full meals in the restaurant, where you can grill your own steak on hot stones.

££ Eight Bells Inn, Church St, Chipping Campden, T01386-840371. Fresh pub food in an old stonemason's lodgings with good real ales.

££ Churchhill Arms, Paxford, nr Chipping Campden, T01386-594000. Superb cooking pulls in the crowds for lunch and dinner to this village pub.

Cheltenham *p55, map p56*
£££ Lumière, Clarence Pde, T01242-222200. Imaginative British seasonal food and a good selection for vegetarians. 9-course tasting menus are also available.

£££ Monty's Brasserie & Cocktail Bar, George Hotel, St George's Rd, T01242-227678. This modern and popular brasserie offers a good seafood menu.

££ Daffodil, 18 Suffolk Pde, T01242-7000055. One of the city's more lively venues, in an airy converted art deco cinema with good British food and live jazz on Mon nights and Sat lunchtimes.

££ Prithvi, Bath Rd, T01242-226229. Refined and sophisticated Indian food; not your average curry house.

££-£ Thai Emerald, St George's Place, T01242-541318. Popular Thai restaurant.

Gloucester p57

££ C&W's African Restaurant, 8-10 St Catherine St, T01452-387911. Offering a selection of dishes from the African continent, the food here is highly rated.

£ Na Lampang, 12 Kingsholm Rd, T01452-382970. A popular Thai restaurant; small but the food is highly rated.

South Cotswolds p59

££ The Bear Inn, George St, Bisley, near Stroud, T01452-770265. Excellent home-made food in this cosy village pub. Check out the Roman well in the village.

££ Daneway Inn, Sapperton, T01285-760297. A delightful old pub near the western end of the Sapperton tunnel.

££ Trouble House Inn, Tetbury, T01666-502206. A superb pub restaurant.

✪ Entertainment:

Cheltenham p55, map p56

The Everyman Theatre, Regent St, T01242-572573, www.everymantheatre.org.uk. Has been hosting stage events since 1891.

The Screening Rooms, The Brewery, Oxford Passage, T0871-2204443, www.thescreeningrooms.co.uk. A luxury cinema with a bar, deli-style nibbles and at-seat service for food and drink.

✪ Festivals

Cheltenham p55, map p56

Mar Cheltenham National Hunt Festival. The Cheltenham Gold Cup is the nation's most prestigious steeplechase. There are also important meetings in **Nov**.

Jul Cheltenham Festival of Music. A big festival, started in 1945 like the Edinburgh Festival, mainly classical.

Cheltenham Festival of Literature in **Oct**, also an oldie, one of the longest-running in the world. Also Jazz in **May**, Science in **Jun** and Folk in **Feb**, all using a variety of venues around the town, including the Pump Room, Town Hall,

Everyman Theatre and various restaurants, pubs and bars. For further information, call the Festivals line on T01242-511211, www.cheltenhamfestivals.com.

✪ Transport

North Cotswolds p51
Bicycle

Cotswold Country Cycles, Longlands Farm Cottage, Chipping Campden, T01386-438706, www.cotswoldcountrycycles.com, Apr-Oct daily 0930-dusk.

Taxi

Cotswold Private Hire, 3 Wolds End Cl, Chipping Campden, T01386-840500. Taxis and private hire.

Cotswold Taxi, Moreton-in-Marsh, T07710-117471 (mob).

Cheltenham and Gloucester p55
Bicycle

Compass Holidays, Queens Rd, Cheltenham, T01242-250642, www.compass-holidays.com; **Forest Adventure**, Coleford, T01594-835116, www.forestadventure.co.uk.

Bus

National Express, T08717-818178, run regular direct services from **London Victoria** to Gloucester (3 hrs 30 mins), from Leeds and Sheffield to Gloucester and from Devon and Cornwall to Gloucester.

Car

Enterprise, 1 Empire Way, Bristol Rd, Gloucester, T01452-419222; **Jackies Self Drive Hire**, The Old Airfield, Gloucester, T01452-720666; **Sixt Car Hire**, Kingsditch Ln, Cheltenham, T0844-248 6620; **Thrifty Car Rental**, Bristol Rd, Gloucester, T01452-383866.

Taxi

ABC Private Hire, 61 Hartland Rd, Gloucester, T01452-424369; **John's Private Hire**, Unit 7a, Woodcock Trading Estate, 277 Barton

St, Gloucester, T01452-385050; **Central Taxis**, Royal Well Rd, Cheltenham, T01242-228877; **A2B Private Hire**, 12 St James St, Cheltenham, T01242-580580.

Train

First Great Western, T0845-700 0125, www.firstgreatwestern.co.uk, run the regular services direct from Gloucester to **Bristol Temple Meads** and **Bath Spa**. There is also a regular service to **London Paddington**.Virgin Trains, T08707-891234, www.virgintrains.co.uk, run the regular direct service to **Cardiff Central** and **Birmingham New St**.

❶ Directory

North Cotswolds *p51*
Medical facilities Moreton-in-Marsh **District Hospital**, T01608-650456.

Cheltenham and Gloucester *p55*
Medical facilities Cheltenham and **Gloucester Nuffield Hospital**, Hatherley La, Cheltenham, T01242-246500.

Contents

Bath & around

Quite a serious contender for top prize in the beautiful cities of Britain pageant, Bath attracts crowds in thousands during the summer. If arriving by rail, first impressions will be of the newest developments in the city, although it only takes a five-minute walk north to begin to appreciate what all the fuss is about. Better perhaps to approach the city from north or south by bike, when it suddenly reveals itself spread out below in all its honey-stoned glory, nestling in a wooded loop of the Avon valley and cradled by seven hills. Eighteenth-century fashionable society's mania for the place is what makes it a sight to behold, the highlights of their architectural legacy being the neoclassical Palladian splendours of the Circus, the Royal Crescent and Pulteney Bridge with its famous weir. Most visitors, though, still come to see the thing that's got everyone going for at least the last 2000 years – the only hot springs in the British Isles. After seeping through the Mendip limestone for some 10,000 years, warmed in the bowels of the earth, the waters that gave the city its name have been worshipped, channelled, contained, drained and splashed about in. The Roman Baths remain the main event, one of the country's most popular and intriguing archaeological sites. The city also does a fine line in other museums: fashion, East Asian art, 18th-century property development and interior design, and fine art. And it also just about manages to avoid being a museum itself. Although famously soporific, the city boasts a wealth of distinctive hotels, shops, restaurants and small businesses, and remains resolutely independent of its much bigger brother Bristol, 10 miles downriver.

Arriving in Bath

Getting there
First Great Western trains serve Bath Spa from London Paddington every 30 minutes, direct services taking about one hour 30 minutes. Estimated time from London by **car** is about two hours. Total distance: 116 miles. From London take the M4 west (about 100 miles) exit at junction 18, head south on the A46, and follow signs to the town centre. From London Victoria **coach** station, to Bath Spa **bus** station, Dorchester Street, the coach takes between two hours 30 minutes to three hours 50 minutes. ▶▶ *For further details, see Transport, page 84.*

Getting around
In the absence of Bath chairs, Bath is best walked around at a leisurely pace, although its hills can prove surprisingly wearing on the legs. Local buses are largely unnecessary to take in the town centre but it's worth taking one of the double-decker tour buses for insight into the city's history. Taxi ranks are found outside the train station and the Abbey. Bike in Bath allows users to rent the bicycles found at docking stations in the city centre; payment can be made online at www.bikeinbath.com.

Information
Bath TIC ① *Abbey Chambers, T0906-711 2000 (general enquiries; premium rate) or T0844-847 5256 (accommodation booking), www.visitbath.co.uk, Mon-Sat 0930-1730, Sun 1000-1600.*

History

Celtic legend has it that Bath was founded by the father of Shakespeare's King Lear, Bladud, son of the King Lud who had founded London. Exiled on account of his skin condition, he became a swineherd. Luckily for him, his pigs stumbled on the only hot springs in Britain. Bladud noticed that their skin condition benefited from a wallow in the warm mud and dived in himself. Miraculously cured, he ordered the construction of a city and temple to the Celtic goddess Sul. When the Romans arrived in the first century AD, they must have been delighted to discover this warming reminder of Rome in chilly Britannia. They called the place Aquae Sulis, constructing a temple to their goddess of wisdom, Minerva, and also one of the finest bathhouses in western Europe, almost certainly visited by all their top brass and possibly even by the emperors Trajan and Hadrian. When the Romans left, the Anglo-Saxons seem to have avoided the place, possibly for superstitious reasons, dubbing it Het Bath. It wasn't until the seventh century that they resettled the area, after defeating the Celts at the Battle of Dyrham, and King Osric established a monastery here close to the springs. In AD 973 Edgar was crowned King of all England in the abbey. After the Norman Conquest, the abbey's power and prestige grew and grew; the present church was constructed on the site of the Saxon church in the early 16th century. The collapse of the wool trade and dissolution of the monasteries soon after ushered in another period of decline for the city – despite James II's wife being cured of her infertility after taking a dip here in the 1680s – and the baths became associated with all manner of vice. Queen Anne visited them in 1703 and inadvertently initiated a reversal in the city's fortunes. Enter drop-out aristocrat Beau Nash, who had come to Bath to indulge his gambling habit, but then raised money for new roads and staged concerts of such class in the city that society was soon squabbling over when they should make the two-and-a-half-day coach trip down

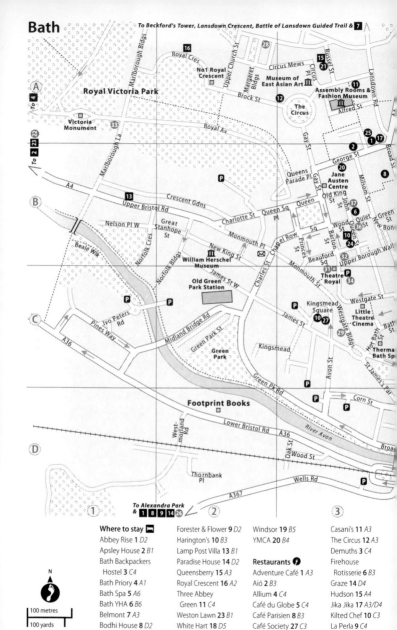

Bath

To Beckford's Tower, Lansdown Crescent, Battle of Lansdown Guided Trail & **7**

Royal Victoria Park

Royal Cres

16
No1 Royal
Crescent

Circus Mews

15
21

Museum of
East Asian Art

Assembly Rooms
& Fashion Museum **11**

12

The
Circus

Alfred St

Victoria
Monument

33

Royal Av

25 **17**
2 **1**

George St

8

Jane
Austen
Centre **20**

Queens
Parade Pl

Old King
St

Crescent Gdns

13

Upper Bristol Rd

Charlotte St

Queen Sq

Queen
Pl

6
37

Wood
St

Quiet

Green

New Bon

10
24

Nelson Pl W

Great
Stanhope
St

Monmouth Pl

Chapel Row

Princes

Barton

Beaufort
Sq

Upper Borough Wall

New King St

James St W

Charles St

Monmouth St

Theatre
Royal **34**

31

**William Herschel
Museum**

Old Green
Park Station

Westgate St

Little
Theatre
Cinema

Bath
St

10
27

Kingsmead
Square

29

Thermae
Bath Spa

Ivo Peters
Rd

Pines Way

Midland Bridge Rd

Green Park St

James St

Kingsmead

Green
Park

Green Pk Rd

Corn St

Footprint Books

West-
morland
Rd

Lower Bristol Rd

A36

River Avon

Broa

Wood St

Thornbank
Pl

Wells Rd

A367

To Alexandra Park
& **1** **8** **9** **14** **26**

① ② ③

N

100 metres
100 yards

70 • Bath & around History

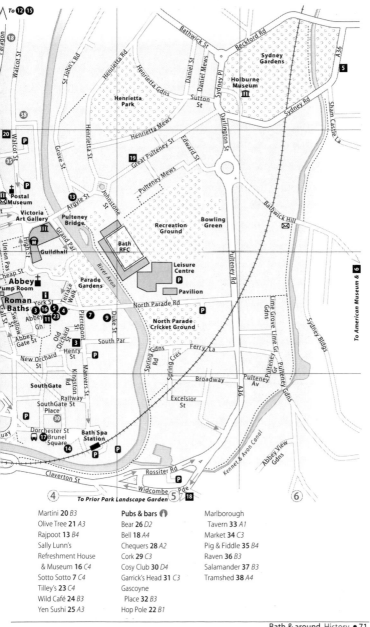

Martini **20** *B3*	**Pubs & bars**	Marlborough
Olive Tree **21** *A3*	Bear **26** *D2*	Tavern **33** *A1*
Rajpoot **13** *B4*	Bell **18** *A4*	Market **34** *C3*
Sally Lunn's	Chequers **28** *A2*	Pig & Fiddle **35** *B4*
Refreshment House	Cork **29** *C3*	Raven **36** *B3*
& Museum **16** *C4*	Cosy Club **30** *D4*	Salamander **37** *B3*
Sotto Sotto **7** *C4*	Garrick's Head **31** *C3*	Tramshed **38** *A4*
Tilley's **23** *C4*	Gascoyne	
Wild Café **24** *B3*	Place **32** *B3*	
Yen Sushi **25** *A3*	Hop Pole **22** *B1*	

from London. In 1738 Beau Nash organized the visit of Frederick, Prince of Wales, under George II (an obelisk with a motto reluctantly penned by Alexander Pope commemorates the occasion in Queen Square) and the city's status as the favourite playground of the beau monde was confirmed. Thanks to the efforts of stone magnate, postmaster and property developer Sir Ralph Allen, grand new Palladian buildings, many of them designed by John Wood and his son, sprang up rapidly all over town and on the surrounding hills. By the time Jane Austen arrived in 1801, Bath was already gracefully going out of fashion but had become an essential stop on the tourist map of Britain, which it remains to this day. Victorians and Edwardians continued to descend on the baths to 'take the cure', which were only closed in the late 1970s, ironically enough because of a health scare. In the 21st century, the city has revived its role as a resort spa with the multi-million pound redevelopment of the old Cross Bath into a health and beauty centre.

Places in Bath → For listings, see pages 79-84.

Roman Baths

ⓘ *T01225-477785, www.romanbaths.co.uk. Nov-Feb daily 0930-1730; Mar-Jun and Sep-Oct daily 0900-1800; Jul-Aug daily 0900-2200; last entry 1 hr before closing. £12.75 (£13.25 in Jul and Aug), concessions £11, under-16s £8.50; combined tickets with Fashion Museum available. Free guided tours every hour; free audio handset tours.*

To this day, the centre of Bath remains its hot springs and Roman Baths, now one of the most popular fee-paying visitor attractions in the country. Expect to have to queue (although it's generally quieter before 1000 and after 1800 in August), but they're well worth the wait. All in all, they provide one of the best insights in northwestern Europe into the Romans' achievement and their remarkably comfortable and sophisticated way of life. The Roman remains only began to be excavated in the late 19th century, and first impressions today are still of the fine 18th-century neoclassical buildings erected on the site at the height of the hot springs fashionable heyday. After looking down into the open-air Great Bath from the Victorian gallery terrace, visitors descend to the water level. The bases of the columns that once supported the Roman roof and the paving stones around the edge of the steaming green tank are the first original features on display, along with the steps descending into the murky depths. If you want to take the free guided tour, it's worth arriving half an hour early to have a look around the museum and Temple Precinct first. As well as the altar, objects on display include the remarkable gilded head of the goddess Sulis Minerva, dug up in Stall St in 1727, some floor mosaics, a model of the Roman buildings' full extent and the Gorgon's Head pediment from the original temple. The entertaining handset audio guide then takes you round the Great Bath, the illuminated East Baths, on to the circular Cold Bath, from where you can look out into the smaller open-air Sacred Spring or King's Bath, the bubbling source of the whole complex. The variety of objects on display mean that a visit could easily last up to three hours, although two would be enough to do it justice.

Pump Room

ⓘ *T01225-444477, www.romanbaths.co.uk. Daily 0930-1600; reservations Mon-Fri; queuing system at the weekends.*

Next door to the entrance to the Roman Baths, the Pump Room is a beautifully proportioned late-18th-century hall overlooking the open-air King's Bath, as much the focal point of the Bath tourist scene today, complete with 'living statues' and buskers outside, as it was during the time of Beau Nash. The Pump Room Trio play every day; check the website for times, presided over by a statue of the dandy himself, and help prevent this quite special restaurant and café feeling like just another tourist trap. The motto 'water is best' is inscribed on the Greek portico courtesy of the Bath Temperance Society, and the spring water itself can be sampled here.

Abbey

ⓘ *T01225-422462, www.bathabbey.org. Mon 0930-1800, Tue-Sat 0900-1800, Sun 1300-1430, 1630-1730. Recommended donation £2.50, students £1.*

Architecturally of just as much interest as the Baths is the Abbey. Building began in 1499 at the instigation of Bishop Oliver King. He had had a dream, depicted in stone on the west front, of angels climbing up and down a ladder reaching to heaven. The highlights of the church's interior are its windows and the Tudor fan-vaulting designed by Henry

VII's master mason, William Vertue, reminiscent of his work in Westminster Abbey. The vaulting in the chancel and choir is original, while the nave's was well restored by Sir George Gilbert Scott in the 1860s. Altogether, the Abbey adds up to one of the finest examples of a purely Perpendicular church in the country, the last to be built in England before the Reformation. The Heritage Vaults beneath tell the history of the site. **Guided tower tours** ① *Nov-Mar daily 1100-1500 on the hour (Jun-Aug until 1700), £6, children £3*, show the bell tower and spectacular views of the surrounding cityscape (but do involve climbing narrow stone staircases).

Thermae Bath Spa

① *Hot Bath St, T0844-888 0844, T01225-331234, www.thermaebathspa.com. Daily 0900-2130. Spa sessions from £26; packages from £69, towel & robe hire extra. Café open 1000-2100.*
A few hundred yards in the opposite direction, across Stall Street, colonnaded Bath Street leads down to five more listed historical buildings that were seriously redeveloped in 2006 into a visitor attraction and centre of interest. Thermae Bath Spa is Britain's only natural thermal spa. The 18th-century **Hot Bath**, the sweet little **Cross Bath** (for private hire), and a rooftop pool offering stunning views over the city are the centrepiece of the development, which also includes **Springs Café & Restaurant**, a spa shop and a visitor centre. The Cross Bath itself lies close to the original Sacred Cross spring. Expect long queues for the spa at the weekends.

Herschel Museum of Astronomy

① *19 New King St, T01225-446865, www.herschelmuseum.org.uk. Mon-Fri 1300-1700, Sat and Sun 1100-1700, closed in winter. £6, children £3, concessions available.*
A five-minute walk west of the Cross Bath, the William Herschel Museum preserves the home of a prominent figure in 18th-century Bath society. William Herschel was an organist, composer and amateur astronomer. In 1781, from the garden of his home here, using a telescope of his own design, he discovered the planet Uranus. The museum is a great find for keen astronomers, and the late Sir Patrick Moore was a patron.

Theatre Royal and Queen Square

At the foot of Barton Street is the Theatre Royal (Sawclose; see page 82), its elegant façade constructed in 1805 and completely refurbished in 2010. Heading north from here will lead you towards the first of three 18th-century set pieces that have justifiably made Bath's architectural legacy world-famous. Queen Square was the first of architect John Wood the Elder's projects, built between 1728 and 1734, beautifully proportioned, right down to the windows (now with their original panes restored), and its north side making up a complete palace frontage. The green space in its centre often hosts boules matches and continental markets.

Jane Austen Centre

① *40 Gay St, T01225-443000, www.janeausten.co.uk. Apr-Oct daily 0945-1730 (1900 in Jul and Aug); Nov-Mar Sun-Fri 1100-1630, Sat 0945-1730. £8, children £4.50.*
A stiff climb up Gay Street passes the Jane Austen Centre. No recreated rooms here, but the museum aims to show how the city influenced her works, especially *Northanger Abbey* and *Persuasion*, and is also home to the Regency Tea Room where you can have 'Tea with Mr Darcy'. Costumed guides pose outside for photographs, and walking tours are also arranged here. The centre also hosts the Jane Austen Festival, held annually.

The Circus

At the top of Gay Street, the second architectural set piece was planned by John Wood the Elder, but carried out by his son and completed in 1767. The Circus was the first of its type in the country and represents Georgian architecture at its most ladylike, with its little balconies (originally painted not black, but dark red and green), delicate columns and arcane decorative symbols, including stone acorns, apparently in honour of Bladud's pigs' favourite food. Thomas Gainsborough moved into No 17, when just starting out on his highly successful career as society's favourite portrait painter. And, in its time, the Circus also accommodated the missionary David Livingstone, General Clive of India and the arctic explorer Parry. Based on the dimensions of Stonehenge, its three graceful crescents surround five majestic plane trees planted in 1804. The garden at No 4 has been restored to something like its Georgian appearance (accessed via Victoria Park).

The Royal Crescent and Victoria Park

A hundred yards down Brock Street, past the chi-chi shopping strip of Margaret's Buildings, the ground opens up in front of the third and most spectacular of the Wood developments. The Royal Crescent sweeps round to the right, facing south over **Royal Victoria Park** and the river valley with views right over to Beechen Cliff beyond. Completed by John Wood the Younger over a period of seven years, its positioning, rhythm, scale and scope still give just as lively an impression of fashionable 18th-century life as any Jane Austen adaptation. And if it's period detail you're after, at **No 1** ① *T01225-428126, www.no1royalcrescent.org.uk, closed for refurbishment, due to reopen summer 2013; check website for details*, the interior of the very grand end house was painstakingly returned to its Georgian condition in the late 1960s. Surprisingly modern in atmosphere, despite the lack of electric light fittings, the dining room on the ground floor, as well as the drawing room and lady's bedroom on the first, would delight the most finicky art director. The 2013 refurbishment will double the size of the museum and reunite the townhouse with its original service wing.

Victoria Park, the green space in front of the Crescent, is a popular place to relax and picnic in summer, and is home to a bandstand, botanical gardens, golf and tennis facilities, and a great children's playground, and is the departure point for hot air balloon rides.

Museum of East Asian Art

① *12 Bennett St, T01225-464640, www.meaa.org.uk. Tue-Sat 1000-1700 (last admission 1630), Sun 1200-1700. £5, £children £3.50, concessions available.*

Back in the Circus, Bennett Street leads northeast past the Museum of East Asian Art, which devotes three floors to treasures from East and Southeast Asia, dating from 5000 BC to the present day, with an extensive collection of Chinese jade and ceramics, as well as gourds, sculpture, including ivory and bamboo carvings.

Assembly Rooms and The Fashion Museum

① *Bennett St, T01225-477173. Nov-Feb daily 1030-1700, Mar-Oct daily 1030-1800, £2.*

The Assembly Rooms, once the social hub of the city, are now owned by the National Trust. The Ball Room, Octagon, Tea Room and Card Room are the public rooms designed by John Wood the Younger in 1769 that have been restored, including the nine great chandeliers. The Ball Room is now utilised by the **Fashion Museum** ① *T01225-477789, www.fashionmuseum.co.uk, opening times as per Assembly Rooms, £7.75, children £5.75, family £22; joint ticket with Roman Baths available* which also extends into the basement. Previously known as the Museum of Costume, it was revamped in 2007 and is one of the greatest collections of historical and fashionable dress. Exhibits change constantly; check the website for details of what's on.

Building of Bath Museum

ⓘ *T01225-333895, www.buildingofbathcollection.org.uk. Tue-Fri 1400-1700, Sat and Sun 1030-1700, £5, children £2.50 concessions £4.*

Round the corner off Guinea Lane, on the Paragon, is an 18th-century Gothic chapel commissioned by the Methodist evangelist Selina, Countess of Huntingdon. (Her face in a portrait reminded Edith Sitwell of 'a fillet of boiled plaice'.) Here, visitors can gain an understanding of exactly how the city was developed. The Building of Bath Museum gives the full low-down on the construction of 18th-century Bath, how it came to look the way it does, as well as how it was decorated and inhabited, with models, architects' drawings and paintings in the Building gallery, and engravings, house plans, gilding and cabinet-work in the Interiors gallery.

Postal Museum

ⓘ *27 Northgate St, T01225-460333, www.bathpostalmuseum.co.uk. Mon-Sat 1100-1700 (1630 in winter), £3.50, children £1.50, concessions available.*

Heading back toward the city centre above the banks of the Avon, the Postal Museum celebrates the honour of being the place where the first postage stamp in the world was used on 2 May 1840, and illustrates '4000 years of communication from clay mail to e-mail'. It's also in honour of Ralph Allen, Bath's first postmaster, quarryman and general bigwig, who invented a system whereby letters weren't forced to go via London to reach the rest of the country.

Pulteney Bridge

Walcot Street continues south into the High Street, back into the boundaries of the medieval city. To the left, down Bridge Street, stands another unmissable piece of 18th-century architecture in the city. Pulteney Bridge was designed by Robert Adam in the early 1770s and is unique in the country for still being lined with its original booths for shopkeepers. Along with the famous horseshoe weir on the Avon, it provides one of the most popular images of Bath. The bridge is best seen from North Parade, but a walk across it is mandatory in order to appreciate the splendour of Great Pulteney Street. The widest in Europe when it was built, wide enough for a horse and carriage to turn without having to back up, it provided the inspiration for the dimensions of the Champs Elysées. Up to the right are the old pleasure gardens of Henrietta Park.

Holburne Museum

ⓘ *T01225-388569, www.holburne.org. Mon-Sat 1000-1700, Sun 1100-1700, free (charge for temporary exhibitions).*

In a commanding position at the end of Great Pulteney Street, the Holburne Museum in a former 18th-century hotel is the appropriately elegant setting for the fine art collection of 19th-century collector Sir William Holburne. It features a number of Old Masters, as well as silver, porcelain, furniture and portrait miniatures (including one of Beau Nash), alongside a strong showing from great English landscape and portrait painters like Turner and Gainsborough. A large, modern, glass extension was added and opened in May 2011, which means new galleries now display 60% more of the collection. There is also a lovely Garden Café.

Sydney Gardens

Behind the museum stretch the leafy Sydney Pleasure Gardens, crossed by Brunel's railway and with ornate bridges over the Kennet and Avon Canal. Jane Austen lived at no 4 Sydney Place for three years, and there are views of the Sham Castle built by Sir Ralph Allen to provide a romantic view from his house on North Parade in 1760.

Victoria Art Gallery

ⓘ *Bridge St, T01225-477233, www.victoriagal.org.uk. Tue-Sat 1000-1700, Sun 1330-1700, free.*
Back on Bridge Street, near the High Street, the Victoria Art Gallery is a fairly straightforward municipal art gallery with a good permanent exhibition of European art from about 1500 to present day and regular temporary shows by local artists and touring collections of interest. A few doors down on the High Street, the **Guildhall** contains perhaps the finest Georgian public rooms in the city, in Robert Adam style with superb chandeliers and a selection of royal portraits.

With more time, a few places just beyond the city are well worth seeking out. To the north, a couple of miles up Lansdown Road, **Beckford's Tower** ⓘ *Lansdown Rd, T01225-460705, Easter-Oct, Sat, Sun and bank hols 1030-1700, £4, children £1.50, concessions £3, family £9,* stands in the Lansdown Burial Ground, the last surviving monument to the huge wealthy and eccentric early champion of the neo-Gothic architectural style eventually beloved by the Victorians. William Beckford had this Italianate tower built in 1827, as a kind of mausoleum. There are great views over the countryside from the little belvedere at the top (Bristol and the Severn are visible on a clear day) but unfortunately not over Bath itself. The belvedere has been lovingly restored to its original condition and in the rooms downstairs, a small museum pays tribute to Beckford and includes a model of his fantastic house at Fonthill (no longer standing). (If you want decent views of the city, head for **Lansdown Crescent**, another sweeping crescent, designed by John Palmer in the early 1790s, on the way back into the city.)

On the other side of the city, via Bathwick Hill, is the **American Museum** ⓘ *Claverton Manor, T01225-460503, www.americanmuseum.org, Mar-Nov Tue-Sun 1200-1700, also Mon in Aug, £9, children £5, concessions £8, garden only £5.50, children £3.30, concessions £4.50.* North Americans may find this place faintly patronizing – a bit like coming across an English Museum in California full of bowler hats and brollies – but it's one of the oldest museums dedicated to Americana in the country. Assembled into a series of period-furnished rooms from colonial times up to the Civil War, it includes displays of Shaker furniture, some remarkable quilts, Native American artefacts, and much else. In the grounds, the copy of Washington's garden in Virginia is apparently pretty authentic. A free shuttle bus service to the museum runs from the city centre, leaving from Terrace Walk (Bog Island).

To the southeast, some of the finest views of the city from afar can be had at **Prior Park Landscape Garden** ⓘ *Ralph Allen Dr, T01225-833422, Apr-Oct daily 1000-1730, Nov-Mar weekends 1000-1730, £5.65, children £3.15, family £14.40,* designed by Alexander Pope and Capability Brown for Sir Ralph Allen, one of the city's most industrious supporters. Prior Park mansion has long been a school, but the beautiful grounds, now in the care of the National Trust, include a Palladian bridge and three lakes. To get there, head south across the river from the centre into Widcombe and, from the White Hart pub, either head straight up Ralph Allen Drive or, if on foot, take a detour through the old village, up Widcombe Hill and along Church Street, before joining Ralph Allen Drive.

For possibly the best view of Bath make your way south of the river and walk up the Holloway, an attractive but steep climb up what used to be the main route into the city, towards Bear Flat. Once in Bear Flat take a left up Shakespeare Avenue and you will arrive at **Alexandra Park**. The views are wonderful, and when the sun shines on the city it looks like a toy town. You can descend through the houses enjoying a bit of Bath's Victorian architecture and day-to-day life.

One of the great pleasures of Bath is to stroll along the towpath of the **Kennet and Avon Canal**, which runs all the way from Bristol to Reading. You can join the canal at the basin by the *Hilton* hotel (just off the A36, Rossiter Road) or a bit further on, by the bridge on Bathwick Hill, and follow your nose east as far as you like. A good stopping-off point is **The George Inn** at Bathampton. More energetic souls can continue all the way to Avoncliff (about an hour by bike), where the Cross Guns pub does decent grub and has a beer garden overlooking the river (see page 84 for bike hire).

Bath and around listings

For hotel and restaurant price codes and other relevant information, see pages 10-13.

⊖ Where to stay

Bath *p68, map p70*
Accommodation prices vary widely according to the season. Central options are either budget or top-end, and both should be booked well in advance during the summer tourist season. 2 new hotels are currently being planned. At the budget end of the spectrum, a **Premier Inn** is due to open on James St West in 2013; in addition, the 5-star **Gainsborough Hotel** on Lower Borough Walls is due to finish construction in 2014 and will be the country's first natural spa hotel.

££££ Bath Priory Hotel, Weston Rd, beyond the Royal Victoria Park, T01225-331922, www.thebathpriory.co.uk. A comfortable place, with spa facilities, garden and charming drawing room (great for afternoon teas) and Michelin-starred cooking in the dining room.

££££ Bath Spa Hotel, Sydney Rd, T0844-879 9106, www.macdonaldhotels.co.uk. Plush, comfortable spa hotel set in 7 acres of gardens. Rooms at the front have good views. Facilities include 2 restaurants, car valeting service and an excellent health and leisure spa.

££££ Lucknam Park, Colerne, east of Bath, T01225-742777, www.lucknampark. co.uk. Famous spa and country house hotel, approached through a mile-long avenue of beech trees, with haute cuisine in its restaurant and a family atmosphere.

££££ Royal Crescent Hotel, 16 Royal Cres, T01225-823333, www.royalcrescent.co.uk. The smartest hotel in the city is located at the smartest address, bang in the middle of its grandest architectural feature, with quiet back gardens and Roman-style spa facilities, oozing discreet Georgian elegance.

££££-£££ Queensberry Hotel, Russell St, T01225-447928, www.thequeensberry. co.uk. Stunning series of townhouses that are only marginally less grand than the Royal Crescent. It incorporates the very well-respected *Olive Tree* restaurant and a courtyard garden for summer drinks behind.

£££ Apsley House Hotel, 141 Newbridge Hill, T01225-336966, www.apsely-house. co.uk. Once the Duke of Wellington's house is now a welcoming family home on the main road, some 20 mins from the centre, with parking.

£££ Paradise House, 86-88 Holloway, T01225-317723, www.paradise-house.co.uk. Large and grand 11-room guesthouse with spectacular garden giving good views over the city, 5 mins' walk from the station.

£££ Three Abbey Green, 3 Abbey Green, T01225-428558, www.threeabbeygreen. com. 7 beautiful rooms in one of the prettiest parts of the town centre.

£££-££ Harington's Hotel, 8 Queen St, T01225-461728, www.haringtonshotel. co.uk. Charming and very central townhouse hotel with modern rooms.

£££-££ Windsor Guest House, 69 Great Pulteney St, T01225-422100, www. bathwindsorguesthouse.co.uk. A refurbished 200-year-old building in a superb position.

££ Abbey Rise, 97 Wells Rd, T01225-316177, www.abbeyrise.co.uk. 3-room Victorian guesthouse with good views over the city from the south, on a main road but convenient for the train station.

££ Belmont, 7 Belmont, Lansdown Rd, T01225-423082, www.belmontbath.co.uk. Spacious guesthouse, 10 mins' walk uphill from the Royal Crescent.

££ Bodhi House, 31a Englishcombe Ln, T01225-461990, www.bodhihouse. co.uk. Eco-friendly B&B offering stylish accommodation with stunning views, just outside the town centre.

££ The Forester and Flower, 172 Bradford Rd, Combe Down, Bath, T01225-837671, www.foresterandflower.com. Quirky and quiet pub that offers B&B accommodation. At least a 30-min walk to the town centre, but there is a bus stop right across the road.

££ Weston Lawn, Lucklands Rd, Weston, T01225-421362, www.westonlawn.co.uk. Friendly, traditional 3-room B&B in an elegant Georgian family home 20 mins' walk from city centre. There are fresh flowers in the very comfortable rooms, and breakfast with home-baked bread is served in the conservatory overlooking a delightfully pretty garden.

£ Lamp Post Villa, 3 Crescent Gdns, Upper Bristol Rd, T01225-331221, www.lamppostvilla.co.uk. Little B&B at the bottom of Victoria Park, on the main road but quiet nonetheless. Luxury Jaguar available for chauffeur-driven tours.

£ Bath Backpackers Hostel, 13 Pierrepont St, T01225-446787, www.hostels.co.uk. No frills, 4-10 person dorms, very close to the train station.

£ Bath YHA, Bathwick Rd, T01225-465674, www.yha.org.uk/hostel/bath. Italianate mansion with rooms and dorms, a short bus ride uphill from the station.

£ White Hart, Claverton St, Widcombe, T01225-313985, www.whitehartbath.co.uk. Cosy pub south of the river, within 5 mins of station, providing some of the best-value beds in town. Rooms are basic but extremely close to the main attractions. Excellent food on offer in the pub downstairs.

£ YMCA, International House, Broad St, T01225-325900, www.bathymca.co.uk. Very central basic accommodation in dorms, singles and doubles. Breakfast available for a small extra charge.

⑦ Restaurants

Bath *p68, map p70*
Bath boasts a bewildering variety of places to eat and drink, generally of quite a high standard despite the obvious temptation to make a fast buck. If you know what you want, you're almost sure to find it done well here somewhere.

£££ Hudson Steakhouse, 14 London St, T01225-332323, www.hudsonbars.com. The place to go for prime aged steaks.

£££ The Kilted Chef, 7a Kingsmead Sq, T01225-466688, www.kiltedchef.co. Top-notch contemporary British food, with a good seafood offering, relatively new on the Bath restaurant scene. It has a cosy vaulted dining room.

£££ Martini Ristorante, 8-9 George St, T01225-460818, www.martinirestaurant. co.uk. Italian restaurant that serves traditional dishes cooked extremely well.

£££ Olive Tree at the *Queensberry Hotel* T01225-447928, www.olivetreebath.co.uk. Another serious foodie option in the city.

£££-££ Casanis, 4 Saville Row, T01225-780055, www.casanis.co.uk. Highly-rated French bistro, fusing the traditionally Gallic and the modern.

£££-££ Graze Bar, Brewery & Chophouse, 9 Brunel Sq, T01225-429392, www.bath ales.com. Brand new restaurant and Bath Ales microbrewery in the new Vaults development by the train station. Great for grilled meats and British ales.

££ Aió, 7 Edgar Bldgs, T01225-443900, www.aiorestaurant.co.uk. Specializing in Sardinian food, this restaurant offers delicious seafood, meats and daily specials.

££ Allium Brasserie, North Pde, T01225-805246, www.abbeyhotelbath.co.uk/ allium-brasserie. This new venture within the Abbey Hotel has quickly wowed the locals.

££ Café du Globe, 1a North Pde, T01225-466437, www.cafeduglobe.co.uk. Cosy little Moroccan restaurant serving authentic, tasty dishes and delicious sweet pastries.

££ The Circus Café & Restaurant, 34 Brock St, T01225-466020, www. thecircuscafeandrestaurant.co.uk. Popular family-run restaurant perfectly situated between the Circus and the Royal Crescent.

££ Demuths, 2 North Pde, off Abbey Green, T01225-446059, www.demuths.co.uk. The go-to restaurant for vegetarian dishes that don't compromise on taste.

££ Firehouse Rotisserie, 2 John St, T01225-482070, www.firehouserotisserie.co.uk. Delicious brick oven-fired pizzas and grilled meats. Generous portions and excellent, attentive service.

££ La Perla, 12a North Pde, T01225-463626, www.la-perla.co.uk. Beautiful vaulted Spanish restaurant and tapas bar.

££ Sally Lunn's Refreshment House and Museum, 4 North Parade Passage, T01225-461634. The most famous medieval house in the city, still purveying the buns perfected by French Huguenot refugee Sally Lunn in the 1680s. Candlelit suppers and cream teas. The museum in the basement contains the original kitchen and a cellar full of stalactites and stalagmites.

££ Sotto Sotto, 10 North Pde, T01225-330236. Another cosy subterranean venue, this time Italian. Great fresh food and impeccable service. Booking ahead advised.

££ Tilleys Bistro, 3 North Parade Passage, T01225-484200, www.tilleysbistro.co.uk. Mostly French cuisine with quite an extensive menu.

££-£ Rajpoot, 4 Argyle St, T01225-466833, www.rajpoot.com. Cosy, traditional decor in another vaulted underground restaurant. Fantastic Indian food and winner of several curry awards.

£ Yen Sushi, 11-12 Bartlett St, T01225-333313, www.yensushi.co.uk. Independent, conveyor-belt sushi restaurant with fresh, highly rated dishes.

Cafés

Adventure Café, 5 Prince's Bldgs, George St, T01225-462038, www.adventure.000space.com. Popular with locals and tourists alike. Garden out the back.

Café Parisien, Milsom Place, T01225-447147, www.leparisien.co.uk. A bath institution with a lovely outside courtyard (although sadly no longer as large, as a chain restaurant has taken over the space), great for coffee and a croissant.

Café Society, Kingsmead Sq. Pared-back, trendy coffeehouse serving exemplary coffee, with a fun kids' area in the basement.

Jika-Jika, George St and Brunel Sq, T01225-429903, www.jikajika.co.uk. Hugely popular Bath coffee house, now with 2 venues in the city, owned by rugby stars Lee Mears and Matt Stevens.

The Wild Café, 10a Queen St, T01225-448673, www.wildcafe.co.uk. Tucked away from the crowds, this compact little café serves delicious breakfast and brunch made with quality, fresh ingredients.

Pubs and bars

Bath *p68, map p70*

The Bear, Bear Flat, T01225-425795 www.bearbath.co.uk. Spacious, relaxed and does great coffees as well as the usual bar drinks. The food is good too, especially the River Fowey mussels when they're in season.

The Bell, 103 Walcot St, T01225-460426, www.thebellinnbath.co.uk. A quirky pub with a very unique character – well worth a visit, especially if you like real ales and live music.

Circo, The Halcyon, 2-3 South Pde, T01225-444100, www.circobar.co.uk. Stylish underground bar with 4 rooms, ideal for those trying to get away from the hen-night crowds on a Sat night.

The Cork, 11-12 Westgate Buildings, T01225-333582, www.thecork.co.uk. Trendy pub with a basement that opens until late and a decent-sized garden.

The Cosy Club. A large, quirkily-decorated bar on the 1st floor of the Southgate shopping centre with an outside terrace.

Hop Pole, 7 Albion Buildings, Upper Bristol Rd, T01225-425410. A 10-min walk west of Queen Sq, just below Victoria Park, this locals' pub is worth the stroll. It has a fine selection of ales and an excellent menu. Lovely garden filled with tables, plants, lanterns and a few pagoda-type constructions in which to sit. If you don't want the walk, try sister pub

The Salamander, 3 John St, T01225-428889, which offers the same ales but without the garden. Both www.bathales.com.
Market, Saw Close, T01225-330009. Great-value food and drinks, with an international selection, but the real pull of this pub is the large garden opposite the theatre. **Garrick's Head**, 7-8 St John's Place, T01225-318368, www.garricksheadpub.com, and **Gascoyne Place**, 1 Saw Close, T01225-445854, www. gascoyneplace.co.uk, are pricier options but ideal venues for a pre-theatre drink.
Marlborough Tavern, 35 Marlborough Buildings, T01225-423731, www. marlborough-tavern.com and **The Chequers**, 50 Rivers St, T01225-360017, www.thechequersbath.com. Sister establishments that are the very definition of the term 'gastropub'. Great for food, although at busy times there's not much space for those just wanting a drink.
The Pig and Fiddle, 2 Saracen St, T01225-460868, www.pigandfiddle.butcombe.com. One of Bath's busiest pubs with a real local feel, good atmosphere and popular garden.
The Raven, 7 Queen St, T01225-425045, www.theravenofbath.co.uk. Cosy pub, another one for real ales fans, and serves great pies from local company Pieminister.
The Tramshed, Beehive Yard, Walcot St, T01225-421200, www.thetramshedbath. co.uk. Sizeable bar with a semi-sophisticated vibe, great place to get food and chill out.

Clubs

Moles, 14 George St, T01225-404445. Moles is a popular, but tiny, live music venue on 2 floors. It offers everything from live world music to techno DJ sets, as well as themed nights including the 'Big Cheese' for the tacky but fun-loving. Also boasts an impressive gallery of previous acts for the indie crowd.
The Second Bridge, 10 Manvers St, T01225-464449, www.thesecondbridge. co.uk. Has become a well-established party-spot since it opened in 2007.

⊙ Entertainment

Bath *p68, map p70*
Cinema
The Little Theatre, St Michael's Pl, T0871-902 5735, www.picturehouses.co.uk. Fantastic independent cinema offering arthouse films as well as main-stream screenings. Comfortable and offers a great selection of fair-trade cinema snacks and hot and alcoholic drinks as well as the usual.

Comedy
Komedia, 22-23 Westgate St, T0845-293 8480, www.komedia.co.uk. This comedy club used to be the Beau Nash Picture House, and has retained its lovely art-deco interior. Also does club and cabaret nights, and shows films in association with the Little Theatre cinema.

Theatre
Theatre Royal, T01225-448844, www. theatreroyal.org.uk. West End previews, touring opera, dramas and comedies in the Georgian main house, more experimental work in the smaller Ustinov studio, and great shows for kids at The Egg.

⊛ Festivals

Bath *p68, map p70*
Mar Bath Literature Festival, T01225-462231, www.bathfestivals.org.uk.
May/Jun Bath Music Festival, T01225-462231, www.bathfestivals.org.uk, a very prestigious music festival, spanning world, jazz and classical genres.
Sep Jane Austen Festival, www.jane austen.co.uk/festivalhome, when Austen enthusiasts don Georgian dress to attend Austen-themed events in the city.

⊙ Shopping

Bath *p68, map p70*
Bath is something of a shopper's paradise, with a wide variety of interesting one-offs

and more than enough antique shops. The new **Southgate** development by the train station is the hub for the usual high-street names, but escapes the banality of a shopping centre by remaining a mostly outdoor development. The exception is the undercover Little Southgate, which is home to a small strip of shops that are not mainstream. This leads on to the main drag, which consists of pedestrianized Union St and eventually up to Milsom St. Wander off into some of the side streets, though, and you will find gems such as **Mr B's Emporium of Reading Delights**, 14-15 John St, an excellent independent bookshop; **Tea House Emporium**, 22 Bond St, where you can buy every tea imaginable; and **Coral Quay**, 8-9 New Bond Street Pl, where you can buy fair-trade trinkets from around the world. Just off Milsom St, Milsom Place, previously known as Shire's Yard, is a small redeveloped shopping mall that is home to exclusive boutiques, Jamie Oliver's Deli and unusual pop-up shops.

Northeast of the centre, **Walcot St** is a good browsing ground and is referred to as the 'artisan' centre of the city with shops selling everything from second-hand clothes to quality furnishings. **Topping and Company**, found on the Paragon at the top of Broad St, is another great independent bookshop.

To the north of the centre, **Margaret's Buildings** is a very refined little strip of boutiques for antiques and classy womenswear. Try **Alexandra May**, 23 Brock St, for a sparkling treasure-trove of vintage costume jewellery; **Hansel und Gretel**, at No 9, for imported, twee little gifts and a strudel bar in the basement, and **Uber**, No 6, for Alpine-chic clothing. Go via Bartlett Street for boutiques and homeware, as well as **Itchy Feet**, 4 Bartlett St, an independent retailer of travel gear.

Food
If it's food you're after, then try some of the great delis in Bath, including **The Fine Cheese Company**, 29-31 Walcot St, for top-quality picnic materials aplenty, with more than 150 handmade curds, as well as bread and wine; **Harvest**, 37 Walcot St, T01225-465519, for organic wholefoods. **Paxton and Whitfield**, 1 John St, T01225-466403, a venerable old cheesemonger, and **Chandos Deli**,12 George St, for cheese, meats, antipasti and other treats.

Markets
Green Park Market, T01225-789613. A skilful conversion of the old Green Park station into a covered market, with food stalls, art and crafts from Wed-Sat, antiques on Thu and the original Farmers Market every Sat.

What to do

Bath *p68, map p70*
Boat tours
Bath Boating Station, Forrester Rd, T01225-312900, www.bathboating.co.uk. Skiff and punt hire for river expeditions upstream from Pulteney Bridge to Bathampton; great fun when the weather's good.
Bath City Boat Trips, T07974-560197, www.bathcityboattrips.com. Tour boats cruise downstream from the riverside next to the Rugby Ground.
The Pulteney Princess, T07791-910650, www.pultneyprincess.co.uk. Tours upstream to Bathampton.

Walking tours
Bizarre Bath, www.bizzarebath.co.uk. A comedy walk that leaves the **Huntsman Inn** every evening at 2000 Apr-Sep, £8.
Ghost Walks, T01225-350512, depart from the **Garrick's Head** on Thu, Fri and Sat at 2000, £7.
The Mayor's Corps of Honorary Guides, T01225-477411. Entertaining and free 2-hr walking tours leave from outside the Pump Room throughout the year Sun-Fri 1030 and 1400, Sat 1030 only, and also May-Sep Tue and Thu at 1900.

⊖ Transport

Bath *p68, map p70*
Bicycle
Bath by Cycle, 2 George's Pl,
Lower Bathwick Hill, T01225-
807881, www.bathbycycle.com.
Bath Narrowboats, Sydney Wharf,
Bathwick Hill, T01225-447276, www.bath-
narrowboats.co.uk. Bikes available (as well as
boats). See also Getting around, above.

Bus
First Bus runs the frequent direct X39
service to **Bristol** (40 mins). **National
Express**, T08717-818178, runs the direct
service to **Cardiff** (2 hrs 35 mins), several
direct daily services to **London Victoria**
(3 hrs 20 mins) and a regular service to
Bristol airport (2 hrs), changing at Bristol
bus station. **Traveline**, T0871-200 2233.

Car
On-street 'pay & display' parking is at a
premium in Bath and is expensive. Areas
are clearly signed for 1 hr or 2 hrs maximum
stay. The largest car parks in the town centre
are found at Southgate, off Dorchester St,
or on Charlotte St. If spending a day in
Bath, the best options are the Park & Ride
car parks in Lansdown (from north), Bath
University and Odd Down (from south)
or Newbridge (from west).
    Europcar, Brassmill Ln, T0871-384 9985;
Enterprise, Lower Bristol Rd, T01225-443311;
Hertz, Windsor Bridge Rd, T0843-309 3004.

Taxi
Abbey Taxis, South Pde, T01225-444444;
V-Cars, 11 Cheltenham St, T01225-464646;
Widcombe Cars, 21 Greenacres, T01225-
422610.

Train
First Great Western, T0845-700 0125,
www.firstgreatwestern.co.uk, runs the
frequent direct service from Bath Spa to
Bristol Temple Meads (15 mins), twice
hourly direct to **London Paddington** (1 hr
30 mins) and once hourly to **Cardiff Central**
(1 hr 5 mins). There are also services to
Salisbury and Southampton. **National Rail
Enquiries**, www.nationalrail.co.uk.

ⓘ Directory

Bath *p68, map p70*
Hospitals Royal United Hospital,
Combe Park, T01225-428331.

Contents

Footnotes

Index

Titles available in the Footprint *Focus* range

Latin America	UK RRP	US RRP
Bahia & Salvador	£7.99	$11.95
Brazilian Amazon	£7.99	$11.95
Brazilian Pantanal	£6.99	$9.95
Buenos Aires & Pampas	£7.99	$11.95
Cartagena & Caribbean Coast	£7.99	$11.95
Costa Rica	£8.99	$12.95
Cuzco, La Paz & Lake Titicaca	£8.99	$12.95
El Salvador	£5.99	$8.95
Guadalajara & Pacific Coast	£6.99	$9.95
Guatemala	£8.99	$12.95
Guyana, Guyane & Suriname	£5.99	$8.95
Havana	£6.99	$9.95
Honduras	£7.99	$11.95
Nicaragua	£7.99	$11.95
Northeast Argentina & Uruguay	£8.99	$12.95
Paraguay	£5.99	$8.95
Quito & Galápagos Islands	£7.99	$11.95
Recife & Northeast Brazil	£7.99	$11.95
Rio de Janeiro	£8.99	$12.95
São Paulo	£5.99	$8.95
Uruguay	£6.99	$9.95
Venezuela	£8.99	$12.95
Yucatán Peninsula	£6.99	$9.95

Asia	UK RRP	US RRP
Angkor Wat	£5.99	$8.95
Bali & Lombok	£8.99	$12.95
Chennai & Tamil Nadu	£8.99	$12.95
Chiang Mai & Northern Thailand	£7.99	$11.95
Goa	£6.99	$9.95
Gulf of Thailand	£8.99	$12.95
Hanoi & Northern Vietnam	£8.99	$12.95
Ho Chi Minh City & Mekong Delta	£7.99	$11.95
Java	£7.99	$11.95
Kerala	£7.99	$11.95
Kolkata & West Bengal	£5.99	$8.95
Mumbai & Gujarat	£8.99	$12.95

Africa & Middle East	UK RRP	US RRP
Beirut	£6.99	$9.95
Cairo & Nile Delta	£8.99	$12.95
Damascus	£5.99	$8.95
Durban & KwaZulu Natal	£8.99	$12.95
Fès & Northern Morocco	£8.99	$12.95
Jerusalem	£8.99	$12.95
Johannesburg & Kruger National Park	£7.99	$11.95
Kenya's Beaches	£8.99	$12.95
Kilimanjaro & Northern Tanzania	£8.99	$12.95
Luxor to Aswan	£8.99	$12.95
Nairobi & Rift Valley	£7.99	$11.95
Red Sea & Sinai	£7.99	$11.95
Zanzibar & Pemba	£7.99	$11.95

Europe	UK RRP	US RRP
Bilbao & Basque Region	£6.99	$9.95
Brittany West Coast	£7.99	$11.95
Cádiz & Costa de la Luz	£6.99	$9.95
Granada & Sierra Nevada	£6.99	$9.95
Languedoc: Carcassonne to Montpellier	£7.99	$11.95
Málaga	£5.99	$8.95
Marseille & Western Provence	£7.99	$11.95
Orkney & Shetland Islands	£5.99	$8.95
Santander & Picos de Europa	£7.99	$11.95
Sardinia: Alghero & the North	£7.99	$11.95
Sardinia: Cagliari & the South	£7.99	$11.95
Seville	£5.99	$8.95
Sicily: Palermo & the Northwest	£7.99	$11.95
Sicily: Catania & the Southeast	£7.99	$11.95
Siena & Southern Tuscany	£7.99	$11.95
Sorrento, Capri & Amalfi Coast	£6.99	$9.95
Skye & Outer Hebrides	£6.99	$9.95
Verona & Lake Garda	£7.99	$11.95

North America	UK RRP	US RRP
Vancouver & Rockies	£8.99	$12.95

Australasia	UK RRP	US RRP
Brisbane & Queensland	£8.99	$12.95
Perth	£7.99	$11.95

For the latest books, e-books and a wealth of travel information, visit us at:
www.footprinttravelguides.com.

footprinttravelguides.com

Join us on facebook for the latest travel news, product releases, offers and amazing competitions:
www.facebook.com/footprintbooks.